KNITTING
Wildlife

To the memory of Dian Fossey,
who dedicated her life to the research and conservation
of the Mountain Gorillas of Rwanda.

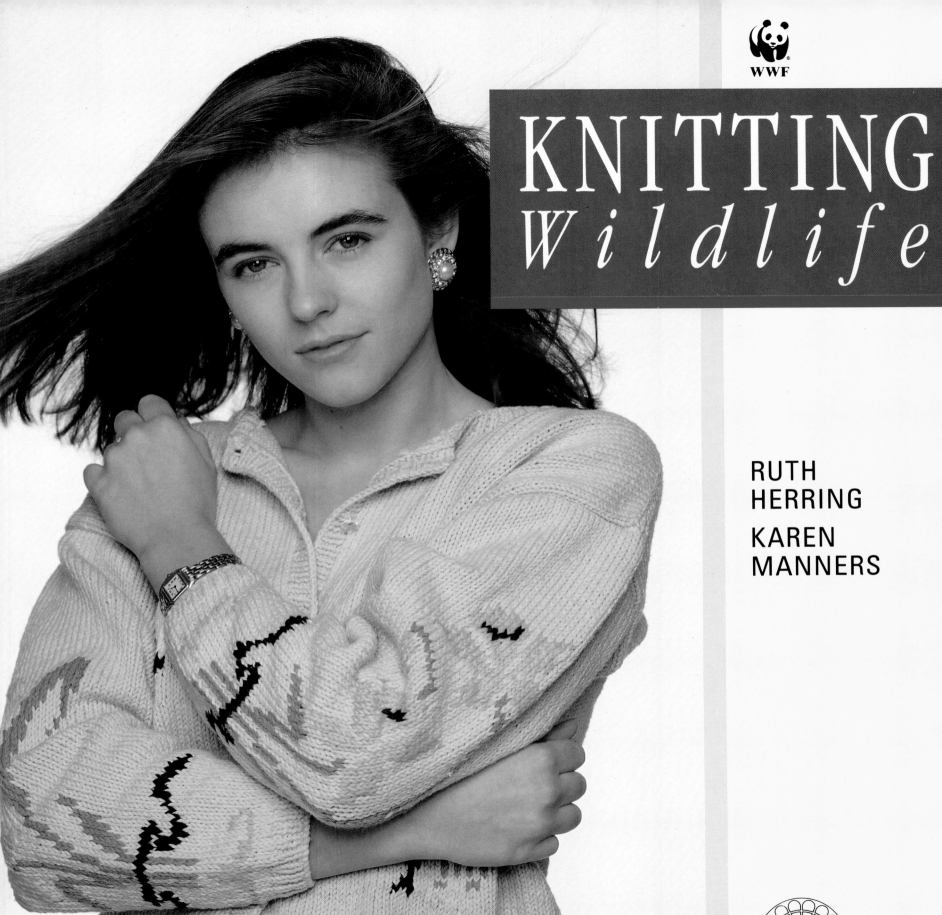

KNITTING
Wildlife

RUTH
HERRING

KAREN
MANNERS

PAVILION
MICHAEL JOSEPH

First published in Great Britain in 1989 by
PAVILION BOOKS LIMITED
196 Shaftesbury Avenue, London WC2H 8JL
in association with Michael Joseph Limited
27 Wrights Lane, Kensington, W8 5TZ

Designed by Janet James
Photography by Kim Knott

A CIP catalogue record for this book is available from
The British Library

ISBN 1 851452346

10 9 8 7 6 5 4 3

Printed and bound in Spain
by Graficas Estella

WWF World Wide Fund for Nature
WWF continues to be known as World Wildlife Fund in
Australia, Canada and the USA.

CONTENTS

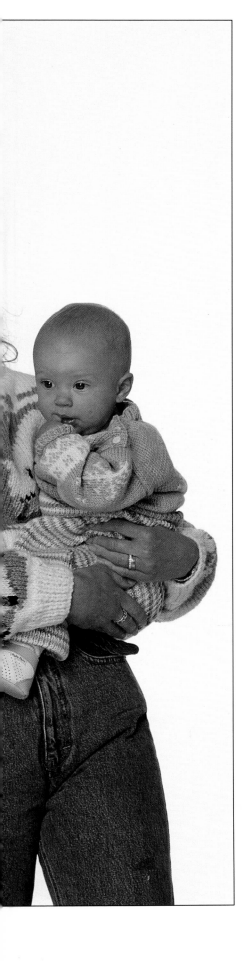

Badgers have suffered at the hands of man for centuries. They have been shot, trapped, poisoned and hunted with dogs. All this in the name of sport, for their pelts and tails which are used to make shaving-brushes, or as alleged crop-raiders, poultry-thieves, or carriers of disease. Their habitat has decreased as woodlands have been cleared and hedgerows ripped up and they constantly run the risk of being killed on roads and electrified railway lines. Unsur- *prisingly they have become rare in several parts of their range, which stretches from Western Europe across most of temperate Asia to Japan. On the whole, however, Badgers are sturdy and adaptable and they are still quite common in areas where they are not excessively persecuted and habitat destruction has not been too great. In such places they can become quite tame and can be a delight to watch playing and feeding in woods and fields.*

BADGERS
and Wildflowers

▶ A timid Badger is seen here peeping through the lush undergrowth of meadow flowers. Chunky yarn is used to create a luxurious and richly coloured box sweater. Worked in two pieces, the stripy welt and collar are added later.

SIZES
One size to fit 80–95cm – 32–38in chest

MATERIALS
Pingouin Chunky
4 × 50g balls Noir (shade 16)
3 × 50g balls Persan (shade 07)
2 × 50g balls each of Blanc (shade 01), Feu (05)
1 × 50g ball each of Bleu Nuit (shade 09), Rose Indien (06)
Pingouin Mohican, flecked chunky
3 × 50g balls each of Souris (shade 11),
Pingouin France + (used double)
3 × 50g balls Violet (shade 26)
2 × 50g balls Soleil (shade 10)
A pair each of 5mm (No. 6) and 6mm (No. 4) knitting needles
Stitch holder

TENSION
13 sts. and 16 rows to 10cm over patt. worked on 6mm needles
Check your tension

NOTES
When working motif, use separate, small balls of yarn. When joining in a new colour, leave an end of about 5cm for darning in later. When changing colour, twist yarns together at back of work to avoid making a hole. If preferred, small areas such as flower centres and green stalks may be Swiss darned. For Swiss darning, see 'Know How' section at back of book.

RIGHT SIDE
** Using 5mm needles and noir, cast on 31 sts.
Rib row 1: K.1 violet, * p.1 noir, k.1 violet; rep from * to end.
Rib row 2: P.1 violet, * k.1 noir, p.1 violet; rep. from * to end.
Rep. these 2 rows 3 times more, then rib row 1 once more.
Inc. row: Using noir, rib 1, m.1, * rib 3, m.1; rep. from * to end: 42 sts.
Change to 6mm needles and work from row 1 of Chart, shaping sleeves by inc. 1 st. each end of 5th and every foll. 4th row until there are 68 sts., then inc. 1 st. each end of next 2 rows: 72 sts.
Next row: Cast on 5 sts., then k. in patt. across these sts. and to end of row, turn.

'Badgers and Wildflowers'
modelled by singer Kim
Wilde. Her sixth LP, Close,
has attained Gold Record
Status in ten countries.
1989 began with her
sixteenth UK top forty hit.
Kim devotes much time to
environmental issues.

BADGERS AND WILDFLOWERS

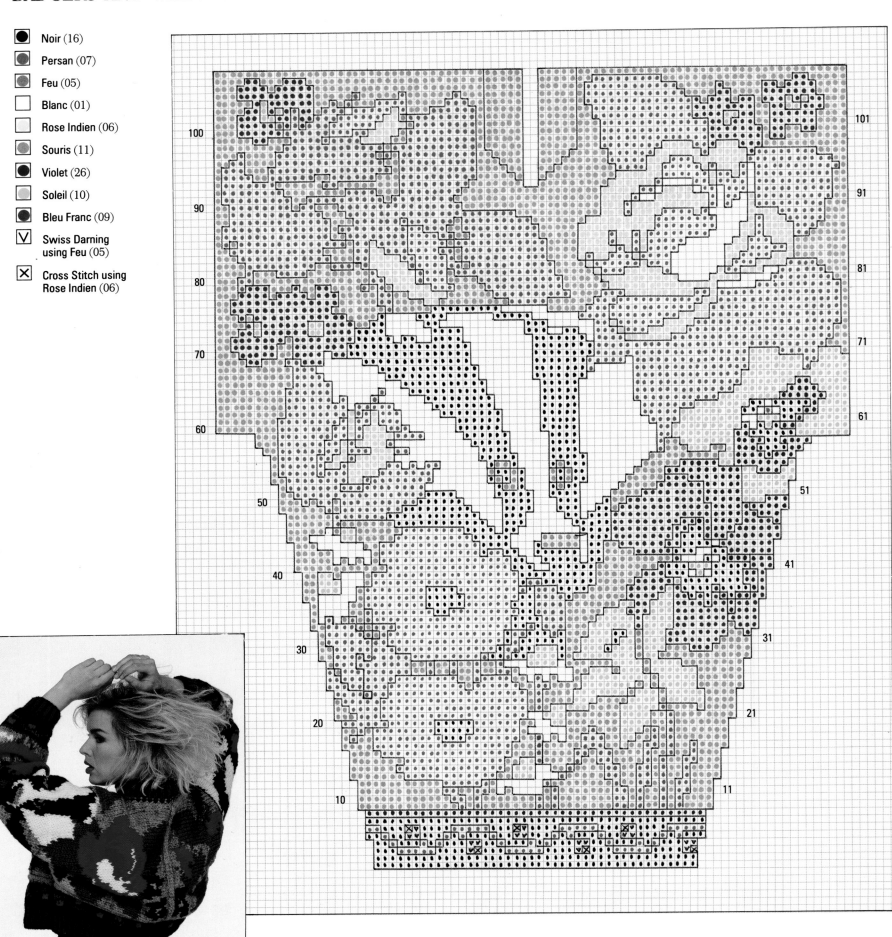

- ● Noir (16)
- ● Persan (07)
- ● Feu (05)
- □ Blanc (01)
- □ Rose Indien (06)
- ● Souris (11)
- ● Violet (26)
- ● Soleil (10)
- ● Bleu Franc (09)
- Ⅴ Swiss Darning using Feu (05)
- ✕ Cross Stitch using Rose Indien (06)

Next row: Cast on 5 sts., then p. in patt. across these sts. and to end of row: 82 sts.

Cont. working straight until row 92 has been completed.

Next row: K.40 sts. in patt., cast off 2 sts., k. to end. **

Back yoke

Keeping work straight, cont. working in patt. on first 40 sts. only until row 108 has been completed from Chart. Cast off. Return to rem. 40 sts.

Shape front neck

With WS facing, rejoin yarn and p.2 tog., p. to end in patt. Cont. working from Chart, dec. 1 st. at neck edge only on every row until 35 sts. rem. Then work straight until row 108 from Chart has been completed.

Cast off.

LEFT SIDE

Work as given for right side from ** to **

Shape front neck

Cont. working on first 40 sts. only, dec. 1 st. at neck edge only on next and every foll. row until 35 sts. rem. Then work straight until row 108 from Chart has been completed. Cast off.

Return to rem. 40 sts.

Back yoke

With WS facing, rejoin yarn to first st. and p. to end. Work straight until row 108 has been completed from Chart. Cast off.

COLLAR

With WS tog., backstitch centre front seam.

Using 5mm needles and souris, with RS facing, pick up and k.36 sts. round left side of neck, 1 st. at centre front seam, then pick up and k.36 sts. round right side of neck: 73 sts.

P.1 row.

Rib row 1: K.1 noir, *p.1 souris, k.1 noir; rep. from * to end.

Rib row 2: P.1 violet, *k.1 noir, p.1 violet; rep. from * to end.

Rib row 3: K.1 violet, * p.1 noir, k.1 violet; rep. from * to end.

Rep. rib rows 2 and 3 twice more.

Using noir, rib 1 row.

Cast off in rib.

Join collar seam, then with WS tog., backstitch centre back seam.

FRONT EDGE

Using souris and 6mm needles, with RS of lower front edge facing, pick up and k.39 sts. to centre front, 1 st. at centre front seam, then 39 sts. to left side: 79 sts.

Cast off purlwise.

Rep. the same for back edge.

JACQUARD AND RIB WELT (Make 2)

Using 5mm needles and noir, cast on 71 sts.

Rep. 2 rib rows as given for right side for 9 rows.

Inc. row: Using noir, * rib 8, m.1; rep. from * to last 7 sts, rib 7: 79 sts.

Change to 6mm needles and work 2 rows noir, then work rows 3–8 from Chart, placing jacquard patt. as follows:

Row 3: K.9 noir, * k.5 persan, k.9 noir; rep. from * to end.

When row 8 has been completed, using souris, k.1 row.

Cast off purlwise.

TO MAKE UP

Block and press pieces lightly under a damp cloth, foll. ball band instructions. With WS tog., backstitch front and back jacquards to cast off edges at lower edge of yoke. Join side and sleeve seams. Embroider cross stitch details on jacquards at cuffs and lower edges as shown on chart.

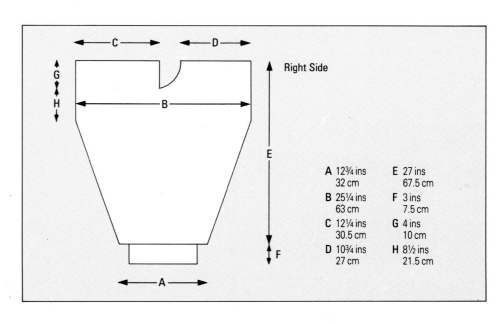

A 12¾ ins 32 cm	E 27 ins 67.5 cm
B 25¼ ins 63 cm	F 3 ins 7.5 cm
C 12¼ ins 30.5 cm	G 4 ins 10 cm
D 10¾ ins 27 cm	H 8½ ins 21.5 cm

The Tiger is the largest of all the cats, and now sadly also one of the rarest. It leads a largely solitary life in the jungles and forests of Asia, hunting down game such as wild pigs and deer. Where these have become scarce, Tigers will turn for food to domestic livestock, and, very rarely, man himself. For this reason, and also for their bones, which are used in traditional medicines, and their valuable skin, they have been relentlessly hunted almost everywhere. Several populations are now extinct while others, such as the Javan and Siberian Tigers, are critically endangered. In total perhaps 3,000 Tigers now survive in the wild, most of these in the Indian subcontinent in India, Bangladesh, Nepal and Burma. In India the 'Operation Tiger' conservation campaign has succeeded in halting the decline, at least temporarily, although the ever-increasing human population makes the Tiger's future even there look far from certain.

White and Indian TIGERS

▶ Dignified and proud, the creature almost comes alive with the use of colour and attention to detail. Choose from the rich golds of the Indian tiger or the pale hues of the rare White tiger. The classic sweater or elegant ladies' suit may be knitted in either colourway.

SIZES
Sweater
To fit 80/85 (90, 95, 100, 105)cm – 32/34 (36, 38, 40, 42)in chest.

Skirt
To fit 85 (90, 95) cm – 34 (36, 38)in hips.

MATERIALS
Sweater (Men's or Ladies')
Emu Superwash DK 100% wool
9 (10, 10, 11, 11) × 50g. balls MS: shade 3019 or 3006
3 × 50g balls Contrast: shade 3070 or 3009
1 × 50g ball each of:
2nd C. shade 3078
3rd C. shade 3012 or 3016
4th C. shade 3006 or 3079

Skirt
3 × 50g balls MS: shade 3019 or 3006
1 × 50g ball each of:
Contrast: shade 3070 or 3009
2nd C. shade 3012 or 3016
3rd C. shade 3006 or 3079

A pair each of 3¼mm (No. 10) and 4mm (No. 8) knitting needles
15cm (6in) zip to match skirt
Stitch holder

TENSION
22 sts. and 30 rows to 10cm over patt. worked on 4mm needles
Check your tension

NOTES
Instructions for larger sizes are given in brackets ( ). When working motifs, use separate, small balls of yarn. When joining in a new colour, leave an end of about 5cm for darning in later. When changing colour, twist yarns together to avoid making a hole.

'White Tiger' modelled by Imran Khan, captain of Pakistan's Cricket team and one of cricket's great all-rounders, hence the title of his autobiography, All-rounder, *which was published last year.*

WHITE TIGER

Men's Sweater

BACK

** Using 3¼mm needles and MS, cast on 107 (113, 117, 123, 129) sts.

Rib row 1: K.1 , * p.1, k.1; rep. from * to end.

Rib row 2: P.1 , * k.1, p.1; rep. from * to end.

Rep. 2 rib rows for 7.5cm ending rib row 1.

Inc. row: Rib 6 (8, 10, 14, 16), m.1, * rib 12, m.1; rep. from * to last 5 (9, 11, 13, 17) sts., rib to end: 116 (122, 126, 132, 138) sts. **

*** Change to 4mm needles and work from row 17 (13, 9, 5, 1) of Chart A until row 162 (166, 170, 174, 176) has been completed.

Shape back neck

Next row: K.48 (51, 52, 53, 56) sts. in patt., turn and leave rem. sts. on a holder. Work on these sts. only.

Keeping patt. correct, cast off 6 sts. at beg. of next and foll. alt. row. Cast off rem. 36 (39, 40, 41, 44) sts.

With RS facing, slip first 20 (20, 22, 26, 26) sts. onto a holder.

Rejoin yarn to first stitch and k. in patt. to end.

Complete 2nd side of back neck to match first side, reversing all shaping. ***

FRONT

Work as given for back from ** to **.

**** Change to 4mm needles and work from row 17 (13, 9, 5, 1) of Chart B, until row 144 (148, 152, 156, 158) has been completed.

Shape front neck

Next row: K.48 (51, 53, 56, 59) sts., turn and leave rem. sts. on a holder.

Work on these sts. only.

Dec. 1 st. at neck edge only on every row until 36 (39, 40, 41, 44) sts. rem., then work 9 (9, 8, 6, 6) rows straight.

Cast off.

With RS facing, slip first 20 sts. onto a holder.

Rejoin yarn to first st. and k. to end.

Complete 2nd side of front neck to match first side, reversing all shaping. ****

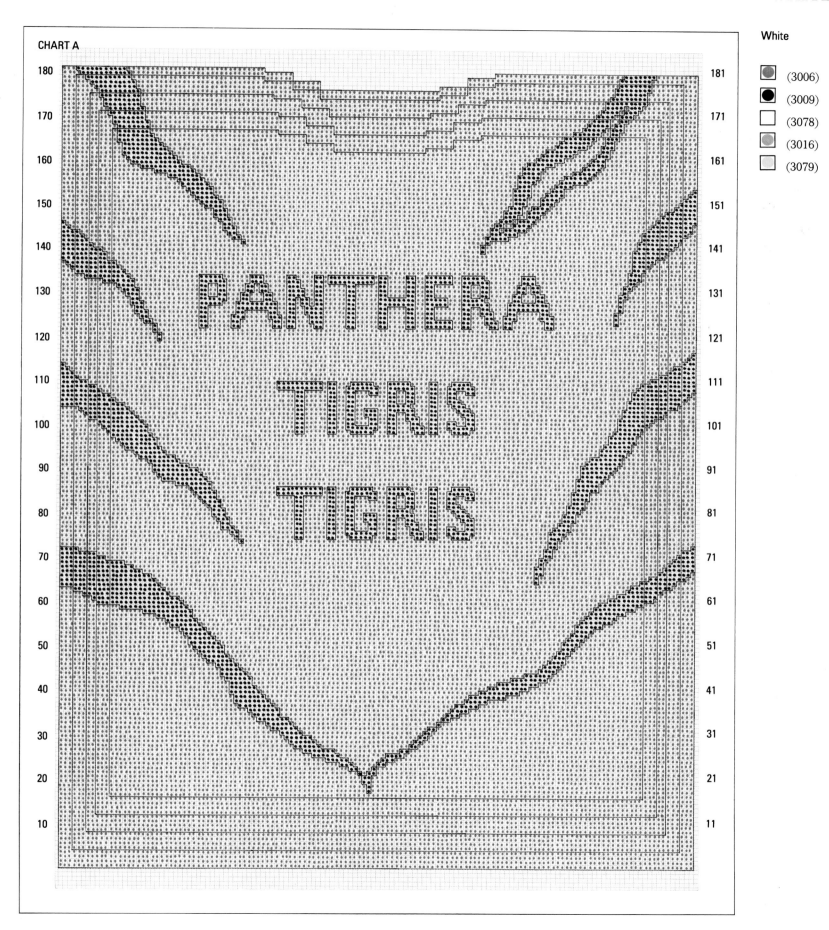

INDIAN TIGER

Ladies' Sweater

FRONT

Work from ** to ** as given for ladies' back, then from ****
to **** as given for men's front.

BACK

** Using 3¼mm needles and MS, cast on 116 (122, 126,
132, 138) sts.
Work 7 rows st.st., ending with a k. row.
Next row (WS): Knit. **
Now work from *** to *** as given for men's back.

SLEEVES (Both versions)

Using 3¼mm needles and MS, cast on 51 (53, 55, 57, 57)
sts.
Work 6cm rib as given for men's back, ending rib row 1.
Inc. row: Rib 6 (6, 2, 4, 4), m.1, * rib 5, m.1; rep. from * to
last 5 (7, 3, 3, 3) sts., rib to end: 60 (62, 66, 68, 68) sts.

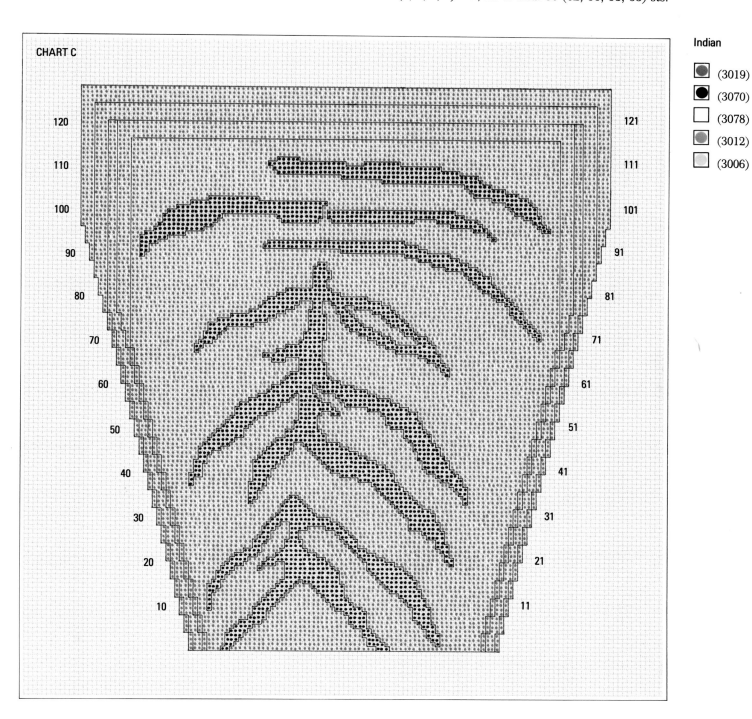

Indian

- ◍ (3019)
- ● (3070)
- ☐ (3078)
- ◍ (3012)
- ◻ (3006)

Change to 4mm needles and work from row 1 of Chart C, shaping sleeves as indicated on chart: 94 (100, 104, 110, 116) sts. When row 116 (120, 120, 124, 128) has been completed, cast off.

COLLAR (Both versions)

Join left shoulder seam.

Using 3¼mm needles and MS, with RS facing, pick up and k.15 sts. down right back neck, k.20 (20, 22, 26, 26) sts. from holder, pick up and k.16 sts. up left back neck, 21 (21, 23, 24, 24) sts. down left front neck, k.20 sts. from holder, pick up and k.21 (21, 23, 24, 24) sts. up right front neck: 113 (113, 119, 125, 125) sts. P.1 row.

Rib row 1: K.2 contrast, * p.1 MS, k.2 contrast; rep. from * to end.

Rib row 2: P.2 contrast, * k.1 MS, p.2 contrast; rep. from * to end.

Rep. 2 rib rows for 9 rows for crew neck or 17 rows for high neck, then using contrast, rib 1 row.

Cast off in rib.

TO MAKE UP

Block and press pieces lightly under a damp cloth foll. band instructions. Join right shoulder and collar seams. Sew in sleeves, then join side and sleeve seams. For ladies' sweater, press hem to inside along foldline and slipstitch in place.

'Indian Tiger' modelled by 1976 'Model of the Year', Marie Helvin, who has worked with Yves St Laurent, Helmut Newton and, of course, David Bailey, with whom she was married in 1975. She is the subject of his acclaimed book Trouble and Strife *and is author of her own book,* Catwalk.

Skirt

Using 3¼mm needles and MS, cast on 76 (82, 88) sts.
Work 7 rows st.st. ending with a k. row.
Next row (WS): Knit.
Change to 4mm needles and work from row 1 of Chart D
for skirt back and Chart E for skirt front, dec. 1 st. at beg. of
row 120: 67 (73, 79) sts.

Change to 3¼mm needles and using MS, work 9cm in k.1,
p.1 rib.
Cast off in rib.

TO MAKE UP
Block and press pieces lightly under a damp cloth foll. ball
band instructions. Join side seams leaving 15cm on left
side for zip. Sew in zip. Finish hem as for ladies' sweater.

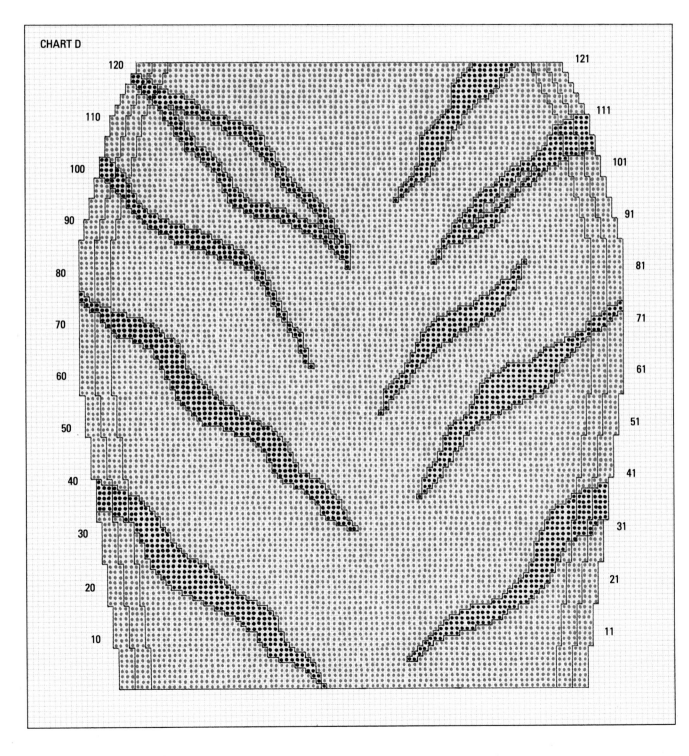

INDIAN TIGER

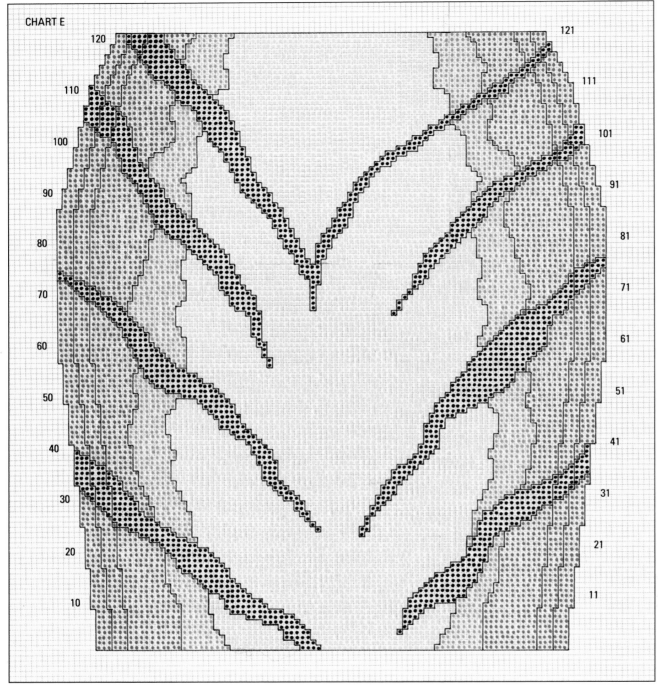

CHART E

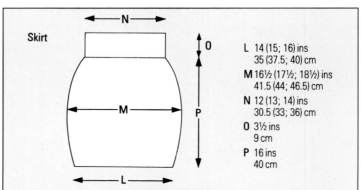

Skirt

L 14 (15; 16) ins
  35 (37.5; 40) cm

M 16½ (17½; 18½) ins
  41.5 (44; 46.5) cm

N 12 (13; 14) ins
  30.5 (33; 36) cm

O 3½ ins
  9 cm

P 16 ins
  40 cm

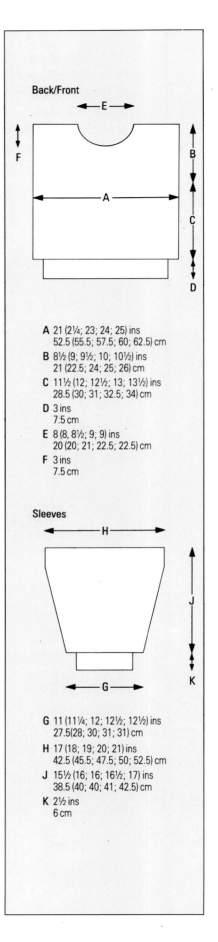

Back/Front

A 21 (2¼; 23; 24; 25) ins
  52.5 (55.5; 57.5; 60; 62.5) cm

B 8½ (9; 9½; 10; 10½) ins
  21 (22.5; 24; 25; 26) cm

C 11½ (12; 12½; 13; 13½) ins
  28.5 (30; 31; 32.5; 34) cm

D 3 ins
  7.5 cm

E 8 (8, 8½; 9; 9) ins
  20 (20; 21; 22.5; 22.5) cm

F 3 ins
  7.5 cm

Sleeves

G 11 (11¼; 12; 12½; 12½) ins
  27.5 (28; 30; 31; 31) cm

H 17 (18; 19; 20; 21) ins
  42.5 (45.5; 47.5; 50; 52.5) cm

J 15½ (16; 16; 16½; 17) ins
  38.5 (40; 40; 41; 42.5) cm

K 2½ ins
  6 cm

Despite their enormous strength and imposing appearance, Gorillas, mankind's closest living relatives, are generally harmless and peaceable creatures. Three distinct populations live in different parts of the great central African rainforests. The Western Lowland Gorilla inhabits forest in Cameroon, Gabon and adjacent countries and numbers perhaps 40,000 in total, but the two others are much rarer. These are the Eastern Lowland Gorilla of eastern Zaire, and the Mountain Gorilla, which lives in the Virunga volcano's region of eastern Zaire, Rwanda and Uganda, and in the Bwindi Forest Reserve in Uganda. The Mountain Gorilla in particular is severely endangered as fewer than 500 now survive. Gorillas everywhere are threatened by the clearing of forests for timber and conversion of land to agriculture, or even, in the case of the Mountain Gorillas, to obtain skulls and hands to sell to tourists.

Mountain GORILLA *of Rwanda*

SIZES
To fit 67.5 (75, 79, 83)cm – 27 (30, 32, 33)in chest.
Age 7 (9, 11, 13) years.

MATERIALS
Hayfield Grampian Chunky
1 × 50g ball each of Black (shade 036024) and Tarn Blue (shade 036063)
Hayfield Lugarno (mohair)
4 × 50g balls Matterhorn (shade 094059)
1 × 50g ball each of St. Moritz (shade 093004) and Champery (093012)
A pair each of 5mm (No. 6) and 6mm (No. 4) knitting needles
Stitch holder

TENSION
14 sts. and 18 rows to 10cm over patt. worked on 6mm needles
Check your tension

NOTES
Instructions for larger sizes are given in brackets ( ).
When working motif, use separate, small balls of yarn.

When joining in a new colour, leave an end of about 5cm for darning in later. When changing colour, twist yarns together at back of work to avoid making a hole.

BACK
** Using 5mm needles and matterhorn, cast on 55, (59, 65, 69) sts.
Rib row 1: K.1 St. Moritz, * p.1 matterhorn, k.1 St Moritz; rep. from * to end.
Rib row 2: P.1 St. Moritz, * k.1 matterhorn, p.1 St. Moritz; rep. from * to end.
Rep these 2 rib rows for 5cm, ending rib row 1.
Next row: Using matterhorn, p.1, m.1, rib to end: 56 (60, 66, 70) sts. **
Change to 6mm needles and using matterhorn, work 62 (66, 76, 82) rows st.st.
Cast off 17 (19, 21, 22) sts., k.21 (21, 23, 25), cast off 17 (19, 21, 22).
Leave centre 22 (22, 24, 26) sts. on a holder.

FRONT
Work as given for back from ** to **.
Change to 6mm needles and work from row 15 (11, 5, 1) of Chart until row 62 (62, 64, 66) has been completed.

MOUNTAIN GORILLA

Shape front neck

Next row: Keeping patt. correct, k.23 (25, 28, 30), turn and leave rem. sts. on a stitch holder.

Work on these sts. only. Dec. 1 st. at neck edge only on every row until 17 (19, 21 22) sts. remain.

Work 7 (7, 8, 7) rows straight. Cast off.

Return to sts. on holder.

With RS facing, slip first 10 sts. onto a stitch holder, rejoin yarn to first st. and k. in patt. to end.

Complete 2nd side of front neck to match first side, reversing all shaping.

SLEEVES (Both alike)

Using 5mm needles and matterhorn, cast on 27 (29, 31, 33) sts.

Work in rib as given for back for 5cm, ending rib row 2.

Inc. row: Using matterhorn, rib 2 (4, 6, 8), * m.1, rib 5; rep. from * to end: 32 (34, 36, 38) sts.

Change to 6mm needles and using matterhorn, work in st.st., inc. 1 st. each end of 5th and every foll. 4th row until there are 50 (54, 58, 62) sts.

Work straight until work measures 30.5 (32.5, 36, 40.5) cm from beg. Cast off.

NECKBAND

Join left shoulder seam.

Using 5mm needles and matterhorn, with RS facing, k. across 22 (22, 24, 26) sts. from holder, pick up and k.15 (15, 17, 17) sts. down left front neck, k. across 10 sts. from holder, pick up and k. 14 (14, 16, 16) sts. up right front neck: 61 (61, 67, 69) sts.

P.1 row.

Starting rib row 1, rep. 2 rib rows as given for back for 9 rows. Then using matterhorn, work 1 row rib.

Cast off in rib.

TO MAKE UP

Block and press pieces lightly under a damp cloth, foll. ball band instructions. Join right shoulder and collar seam. Sew in sleeves. Join side and sleeve seams.

'Gorillas' modelled by
Lydia Raghavan, playmate
of Rory Robertson, who
models the Panda Jacket.

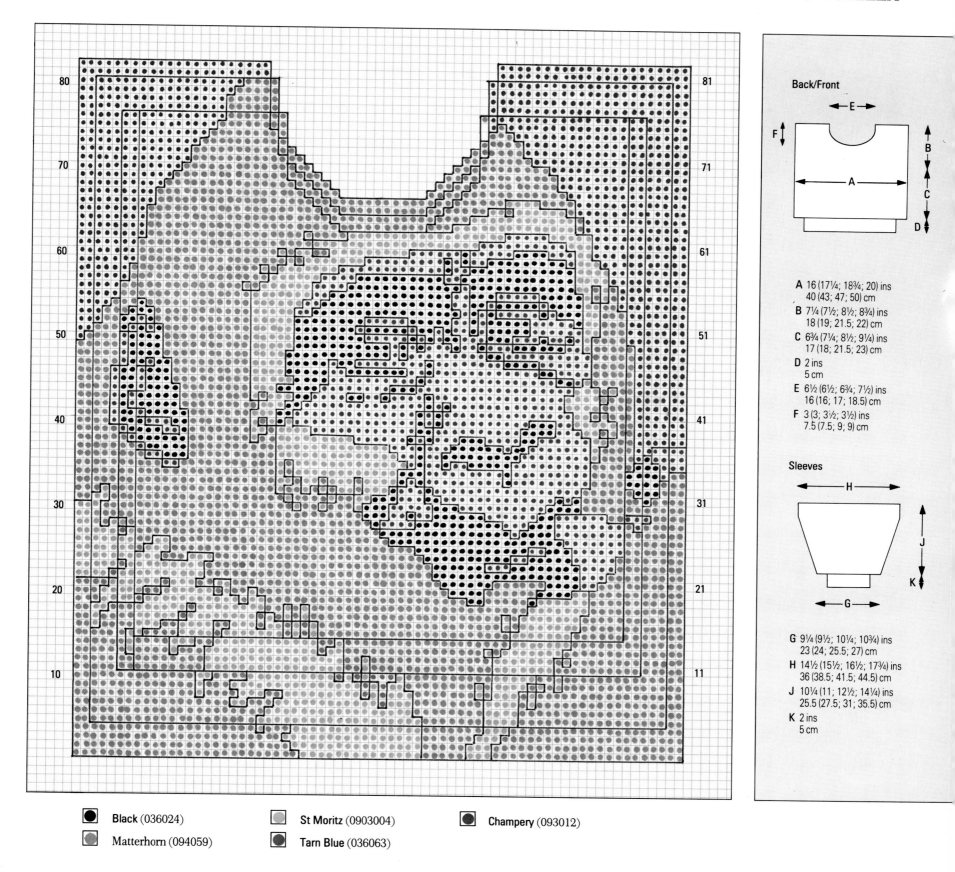

Back/Front

A 16 (17¼; 18¾; 20) ins
   40 (43; 47; 50) cm
B 7¼ (7½; 8½; 8¾) ins
   18 (19; 21.5; 22) cm
C 6¾ (7¼; 8½; 9¼) ins
   17 (18; 21.5; 23) cm
D 2 ins
   5 cm
E 6½ (6½; 6¾; 7½) ins
   16 (16; 17; 18.5) cm
F 3 (3; 3½; 3½) ins
   7.5 (7.5; 9; 9) cm

Sleeves

G 9¼ (9½; 10¼; 10¾) ins
   23 (24; 25.5; 27) cm
H 14½ (15½; 16½; 17¾) ins
   36 (38.5; 41.5; 44.5) cm
J 10¼ (11; 12½; 14¼) ins
   25.5 (27.5; 31; 35.5) cm
K 2 ins
   5 cm

● Black (036024)   ● St Moritz (0903004)   ● Champery (093012)

● Matterhorn (094059)   ● Tarn Blue (036063)

21

The Giant Panda, since 1961 the symbol of WWF, is perhaps the best known and best loved of all rare animals. Fewer than 1300 of them survive in the remote forested hills of south-west China where they are under constant threat from loss of habitat by logging and the spread of agriculture, accidental capture in wild-animal snares, and periodic mass dying-off of the bamboo plants on which they feed. Fortunately, over half of all wild Pandas are protected in twelve reserves set up specially for them. Since 1978 scientists have been studying Pandas in one of the most important of these, Woolong Reserve in Sichuan Province, in the hope that a better understanding of their habits may make it easier to ensure their survival. Plans for the future include the setting up of more reserves, planting of bamboo to provide more feeding areas for Pandas, and reintroducing them into suitable areas where they used to occur.

Giant
PANDA

▶ Sporty designs influence the Giant Panda garments. The adult's sweater features an American football-style motif on the back, whilst the child's, a traditional baseball jacket motif. The Chinese characters mean 'More Effort Needed To Save The Panda'. The bright colours and bold Panda add to the sporty feel.

SIZES
To fit 85 (90, 95, 100)cm – 34 (36, 38, 40)in chest

MATERIALS
Pingouin Chunky
15 × 50g balls Feu (shade 05)
5(5, 5, 6) × 50g balls Blanc (shade 01)
2 × 50g balls Noir (shade 16)
1 × 50g ball Persan (shade 07)
A pair each of 5mm (No. 6) and 6mm (No. 4) knitting needles
Stitch holder

TENSION
13 sts. and 18 rows to 10cm over motif using 6mm needles
Check your tension

NOTES
Instructions for larger sizes shown in brackets ( ).
When working motif, use separate, small balls of yarn.
When joining in a new colour, leave an end of about 5cm for darning in later and when changing colour, twist yarns together at back of work to avoid making a hole.

BACK
** Using 5mm needles and noir, cast on 57 (59, 63, 67) sts. Working in k.1, p.1 rib, work 1 row noir, 11 rows blanc, then 1 row noir.
Inc. row: Using noir, rib 1 (2, 4, 6), m.1, *rib 7, m.1; rep from * to last 0 (1, 3, 5) sts., rib to end: 66 (68, 72, 76) sts. **
Change to 6mm needles and using feu work 32 (36, 44, 48) rows st.st.
Now work from Chart B, placing row 1 of chart after first 16 (17, 19, 21) sts. feu.
When row 10 has been completed, work 14 rows st.st. in feu.
Now work from Chart C, placing row 1 of chart after first 3 (4, 6, 8) sts. feu. When row 16 has been completed, work 16 rows st.st. in feu.

Shape back neck
Next row: K.28 (29, 31, 33) sts., turn and leave rem. sts. on a stitch holder.
Work on these sts. only.
*** Cast off 4 sts. at beg of next and following alternate row. Cast off rem. 20 (21, 23, 25) sts.
Return to rem. sts.
With RS facing, slip first 10 sts. onto a stitch holder. Rejoin

'Giant Panda' modelled by
BA Robertson, composer
and lyricist, and writer of
many international hit
records, the latest being
'The Living Years'. He is
currently producing his
first film for the
Walt Disney Company.

GIANT PANDA

yarn and k. to end: 28 (29, 31, 33) sts.
P. 1 row. Work from *** to end.

FRONT

Work as given for back from ** to **. Change to 6mm
needles and using feu work 4 (8, 16, 20) rows st.st.
Now work from Chart A, placing row 1 of chart after first
10 (11, 13, 15) sts. feu, until row 48 has been completed.

Shape front neck

Next row: K.32 (33, 35, 37) sts. feu, cast off 2 sts., work in
patt. to end.
Next row: P.32 (33, 35, 37) sts. in patt., turn and leave
rem. sts. on a stitch holder.
Work on these sts. only for right front neck.
Keeping patt. correct, ** dec 1 st. at neck edge only on next
and foll. alternate rows until 20 (21, 23, 25) sts. rem. **.
Work 16 rows without shaping. Cast off.
Return to rem. sts. With WS facing, rejoin yarn at centre
front, p to end.
Then work as right front neck from ** to **.
Work 15 rows without shaping.
Cast off.

RIGHT SLEEVE

** Using 5mm needles and noir, cast on 27 (31, 31, 33) sts.
Work 13 rib rows as given for Back.
Inc. row: Rib 2 (4, 1, 2), m.1, * rib 3, m.1; rep from * to last
1 (3, 0, 1) sts., rib to end **: 36 (40, 42, 44) sts. Change to
6mm needles and st.st., work 50 (54, 56, 60) rows feu, 2
rows noir, 14 rows blanc, 2 rows noir, then 2 rows feu, ***
at the same time, shape sleeve by inc. 1 st. at each end of
5th and every foll. 4th row until there are 66 (68, 70, 74)
sts. Then work 9 (17, 19, 19) rows without shaping.
Cast off ***.

LEFT SLEEVE

Work as given for right sleeve from ** to **.
Change to 6mm needles and work 0 (4, 6, 10) rows feu,
then work Chart D placing row 1 after first 11 (14, 15, 17)
sts. feu. When row 47 has been completed, work 3 rows
feu, 2 rows noir, 14 rows blanc, 2 rows noir and 2 rows feu,
at the same time, shape sleeve as given for right sleeve
from *** to ***.

NECKBAND

Join left shoulder seam. Using 5mm needles and feu, pick
up and k.11 sts. down right back neck, k. across 10 sts.
from holder, pick up and k. 12 sts. up left back neck, 43 sts.
down left front and 43 sts. up right front: 119 sts.
P.1 row. Cast off.

Feu (05)   Noir (16)
Blanc (01)   Persan (07)

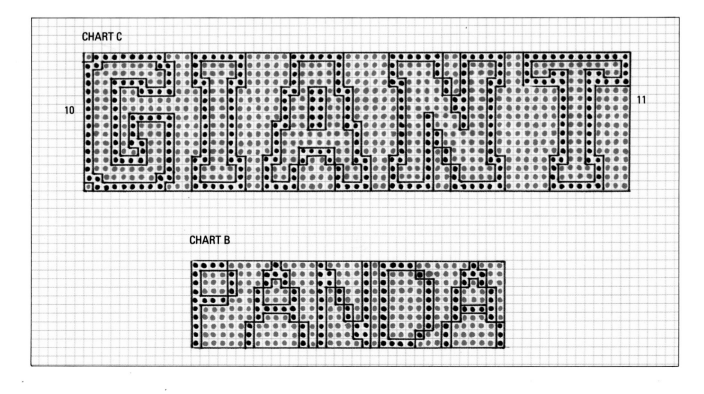

CHART C

10   11

CHART B

24

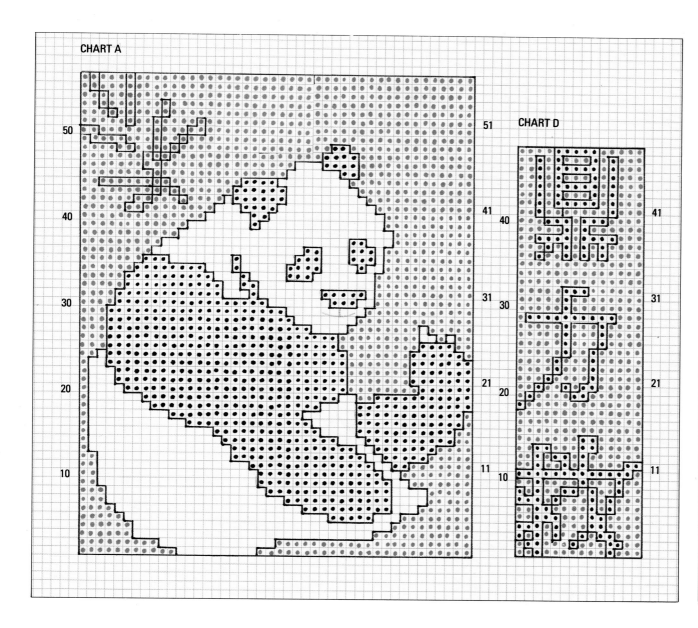

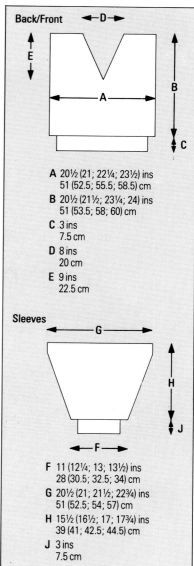

A 20½ (21; 22¼; 23½) ins
  51 (52.5; 55.5; 58.5) cm
B 20½ (21½; 23¼; 24) ins
  51 (53.5; 58; 60) cm
C 3 ins
  7.5 cm
D 8 ins
  20 cm
E 9 ins
  22.5 cm

F 11 (12¼; 13; 13½) ins
  28 (30.5; 32.5; 34) cm
G 20½ (21; 21½; 22¾) ins
  51 (52.5; 54; 57) cm
H 15½ (16½; 17; 17¾) ins
  39 (41; 42.5; 44.5) cm
J 3 ins
  7.5 cm

COLLAR

Using 5mm needles and noir, cast on 119 sts.

Working in k.1, p.1 rib, work 1 row noir, then 12 rows blanc.

Shape collar

Next row: Rib to within 16 sts. of end, yfwd, sl.1, turn.

Next row: yfwd, sl.1, rib to within 16 sts. of end, yfwd, sl.1, turn.

Next row: yfwd. * sl.1, rib to within 6 sts. of last short row, yfwd, sl.1, turn. Rep. from * 9 times more.

Next row: Rib to end.

Next row: Rib across all sts.

Working in rib, work 2 rows noir, 2 rows feu.

Cast off in rib.

TO MAKE UP

Block and press pieces lightly under a damp cloth following ball band instructions. With RS tog., join right shoulder seam and neckband. With WS tog., sew cast off edge of collar to cast off edge of neckband. Wrap left side of collar over right side and stitch in place, folding back edge of left collar. Sew in sleeves, then join side and sleeve seams.

CHILD'S PANDA JACKET

SIZES
To fit 60 (64, 68, 74)cm – 23½ (25, 26½, 29)in. chest.

MATERIALS
Pingouin Chunky
5 (5, 5, 6) × 50g balls Feu (shade 05)
2 × 50g balls Noir (shade 16)
1 (2, 2, 2) × 50g balls Blanc (shade 01)
1 × 50g ball Persan (shade 07)
A pair each of 5mm (No. 6) and 6mm (No. 4) knitting needles
6 × 1.5cm (⅝in) black buttons
Stitch holder

TENSION
13 sts. and 18 rows to 10cm over motif using 6mm needles
Check your tension

NOTES
Instructions for larger sizes shown in brackets ( ).
When working motif, use separate small balls of yarn.
When joining in a new colour, leave an end of about 5cm for darning in later and when changing colour, twist yarns together at back of work to avoid making a hole.

BACK
Using 5mm needles and noir, cast on 45 (49, 51, 55) sts.
Working in k.1, p.1 rib, work 1 row noir, 5 rows blanc, 1 row noir.
Inc. row: Using noir, rib 7 (9, 9, 11) sts., m.1, * rib 8, m.1; rep. from * to last 6 (8, 10, 12) sts., rib to end: 50 (54, 56, 60) sts.

'Panda' modelled by Rory Robertson, first born of proud mother Karen Manners. This is his premier modelling assignment.

Change to 6mm needles and using feu work 2 (8, 14, 20) rows st.st. Now work from Chart A placing row 1 of chart after first 2 (4, 5, 7) sts. feu until row 54 has been completed.

Shape back neck

Following chart for colours, shape neck as follows:

Next row: K.22 (24, 25, 27), turn and leave rem. sts. on a stitch holder. Work on these sts. only.

Next row: Cast off 3 sts., p. to end.

K.1 row. Cast off 2 (2, 3, 3) sts., p. to end.

Cast off remaining 17 (19, 19, 21) sts.

Return to sts. on holder.

With RS facing, slip first 6 sts. onto a stitch holder. Rejoin yarn and work to end. Now complete 2nd side of neck to match first, reversing all shaping.

LEFT FRONT

** Using 5mm needles and noir, cast on 17 (19, 21, 23) sts. Work rib as given for back.

Inc. row: Rib 5 (5, 7, 7), m.1, * rib 4, m.1; rep from * to last (6, 6, 8) sts., rib to end: 20 (22, 24, 26) sts. **

Change to 6mm needles and using feu work 8 (12, 16, 22) rows st.st. Now work from Chart E, placing row 1 of chart after first 2 (4, 6, 8) sts. feu, until row 32 has been completed. Using feu, work 2 rows st.st.

Shape front neck

*** Dec 1 st. at neck edge only on next and every foll. 4th row until 17 (19, 19, 21) sts. remain. ***

Work 9 (11, 5, 5) rows without shaping.

Cast off.

RIGHT FRONT

Work as given for left front from ** to **.

Change to 6mm needles and using feu work 3 (7, 11, 17) rows st.st. Now work from Chart D, placing chart after first 2 (4, 6, 8) sts feu until row 39 has been completed.

Shape front neck

Continuing in patt. from chart, shape neck as given for left front from *** to ***. Work 10 (12, 6, 6) rows without shaping.

Cast off.

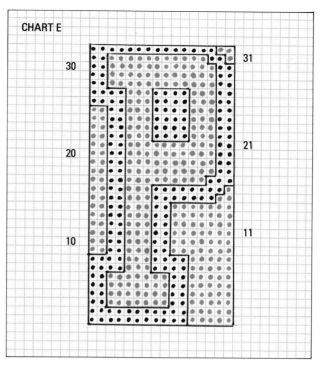

GIANT PANDA

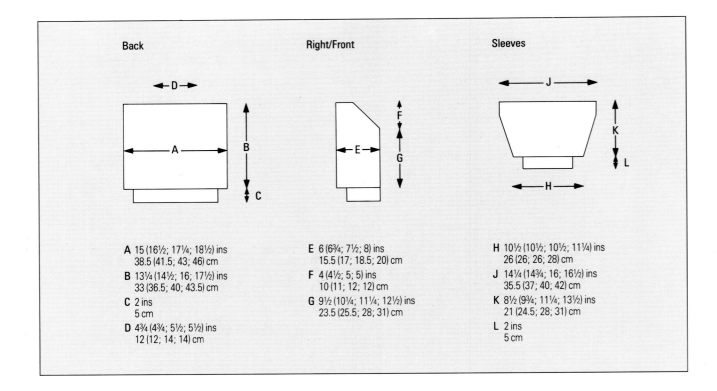

Back

← D →

A

B

C

Right/Front

F

E

G

Sleeves

← J →

K

H

L

A 15 (16½; 17¼; 18½) ins
38.5 (41.5; 43; 46) cm

B 13¼ (14½; 16; 17½) ins
33 (36.5; 40; 43.5) cm

C 2 ins
5 cm

D 4¾ (4¾; 5½; 5½) ins
12 (12; 14; 14) cm

E 6 (6¾; 7½; 8) ins
15.5 (17; 18.5; 20) cm

F 4 (4½; 5; 5) ins
10 (11; 12; 12) cm

G 9½ (10¼; 11¼; 12½) ins
23.5 (25.5; 28; 31) cm

H 10½ (10½; 10½; 11¼) ins
26 (26; 26; 28) cm

J 14¼ (14¾; 16; 16½) ins
35.5 (37; 40; 42) cm

K 8½ (9¾; 11¼; 13½) ins
21 (24.5; 28; 31) cm

L 2 ins
5 cm

SLEEVES

Using 5mm needles and noir, cast on 27 (27, 27, 29) sts.

Working in k.1, p.1 rib, work 1 row noir, 5 rows blanc, 1 row noir.

Inc. row: Using noir, rib 5, m.1, * rib 3, m.1; rep from * to last 4 (4, 4, 6) sts., rib to end: 34 (34, 34, 36) sts.

Change to 6mm needles.

Using st.st., work 22 (28, 34, 40) rows feu, 2 rows noir, 10 rows blanc, 2 rows noir, and 2 rows feu at the same time, shape sleeves by inc. 1 st. at each end of 5th and every foll. 4th row until there are 46 (48, 52, 54) sts.

Work 13 (15, 13, 19) rows without shaping.

Cast off.

RIGHT COLLAR

Join right shoulder seam.

With RS facing, using 5mm needles and feu, start at right front edge and pick up and k.57 (61, 67, 71) sts. to centre back neck.

Rib 14 rows.

Shape collar

Next row: Rib 30 sts., yfwd, sl.1, turn.

Next row: * yfwd, sl.1, rib to end.

Next row: Rib to within 4 sts. of last short row, yfwd, sl.1, turn. Rep. from * 3 times more.

Next row: Rib across all sts.

Cast off in rib.

LEFT COLLAR

With RS tog., join left shoulder seam.

With RS facing, using 5mm needles and feu, start at centre back neck and pick up and k.57 (61, 67, 71) sts. to left front edge.

Work 2 rows in k.1, p.1 rib.

Next row: place buttonholes: ** Rib 2, yon, k.2 tog., * rib 8, yon, k.2 tog.; rep from * once, rib to end **.

Rib 7 rows, then rep from ** to ** once.

Rib 2 rows, then shape collar as given for right collar, reversing all shaping.

TO MAKE UP

Block and press pieces lightly under a damp cloth following ball band instructions. Join collar seam at centre back neck. Sew in sleeves then join side and sleeve seams. Sew on buttons to correspond.

The Arctic may seem a harsh and forbidding place, but in fact it teems with wildlife. Seals, walruses and whales abound in the sea; on land, mammals as diverse as lemmings, arctic foxes, reindeer, musk oxen and polar bears are found, and many bird species migrate here to breed in the brief northern summer. Mankind has not been slow to appreciate this richness and many species have been hunted for food and, often, for their luxuriant fur. As a result some, such as polar bears and musk oxen, have become rare. However, harvest of these is now in general carefully controlled and there is little danger of their becoming extinct in the near future. A more serious long-term threat is the possibility of large-scale disruption of the environment caused by extraction of oil and minerals. Such activities will have to be controlled to ensure the beauty of the area and the preservation of its wildlife.

Arctic
POLAR BEARS AND BABY SEALS

SIZES
To fit 80 (85, 90)cm – 32 (34, 36)in chest

MATERIALS
Pingouin Chunky
6 × 50g balls Blanc (shade 01)
3 × 50g balls each of Ecru (shade 10) and Jeans (shade 19)
1 × 50g ball each of Noir (shade 16), Nuage (shade 12) and Souris (17)
5 × 2cm (¾in) buttons, 1 × 7mm (¼in) clear plastic press stud.
A pair each of 4mm (No. 8) and 4½mm (No. 7) knitting needles
Stitch holder

TENSION
16 sts. and 22 rows to 10cm over patt. worked on 4½mm needles
Check your tension

NOTES
Instructions for larger sizes are given in brackets ( ).
When working motif, use separate, small balls of yarn.
When joining in a new colour, leave an end of about 5cm for darning in later. When changing colour, twist yarns together at back of work to avoid making a hole.

BACK
Using 4mm needles and blanc, cast on 85 (89, 93) sts.
Rib row 1: K.1, * p.1, k.1; rep. from * to end.
Rib row 2: P.1, * k.1, p.1; rep. from * to end.
Rep. 2 rib rows 3 times more, inc. 1 st. at beg. of last row: 86 (90, 94) sts.
Change to 4½mm needles and work from row 1 of Chart A.
Shape armholes by casting off 8 sts. at beg. of rows 31 and 32, then continue working straight until row 72 has been completed: 70 (74, 78) sts.

Shape back neck
Next row: K.25 (27, 29), turn and leave rem. sts. on a stitch holder.
Work on these sts. only.
Next row: Cast off 3 sts., p. to end.
K.1 row.
Next row: Cast off 2 sts., p. to end.
Cast off rem. 20 (22, 24) sts.

▶ This cosy jacket really captures the feel of the Arctic. The all-over design shows masterful males, a female with suckling cubs and on the sleeves, young bears at rest and play. The coal-black features are in sharp contrast to the soft, creamy hues of their coats and the crispness of the white snow and blue sky. Diamanté buttons complete the icy look.

'Polar Bears' modelled by
Angie Rutherford, wife of
Mike.

Return to rem. sts.

With RS facing, slip first 20 sts. onto stitch holder, rejoin yarn to first st. and k. to end. Complete 2nd side of back neck to match first side, reversing all shaping.

RIGHT FRONT

Using 4mm needles and blanc, cast on 49 (51, 53) sts.

Work 2 rows rib as given for back.

Rib row 3: Rib 2, cast off 2 sts., rib to end.

Rib row 4: Rib to buttonhole, cast on 2 sts., rib 2.

Starting rib row 1, work 3 rows rib.

Rib row 8: P.1, m.1, rib to last 7 sts., turn and leave rem. 7 sts. on stitch holder.

Change to 4½mm needles and work from row 1 of Chart B, shaping armhole as given for back at beg. of row 32: 41 (43, 45) sts.

Cont. until row 61 (63, 65) has been completed.

☐	Blanc (01)
☐	Ecru (10)
☐	Jeans (19)
☐	Souris (17)
☐	Nuage (12)
●	Noir (16)

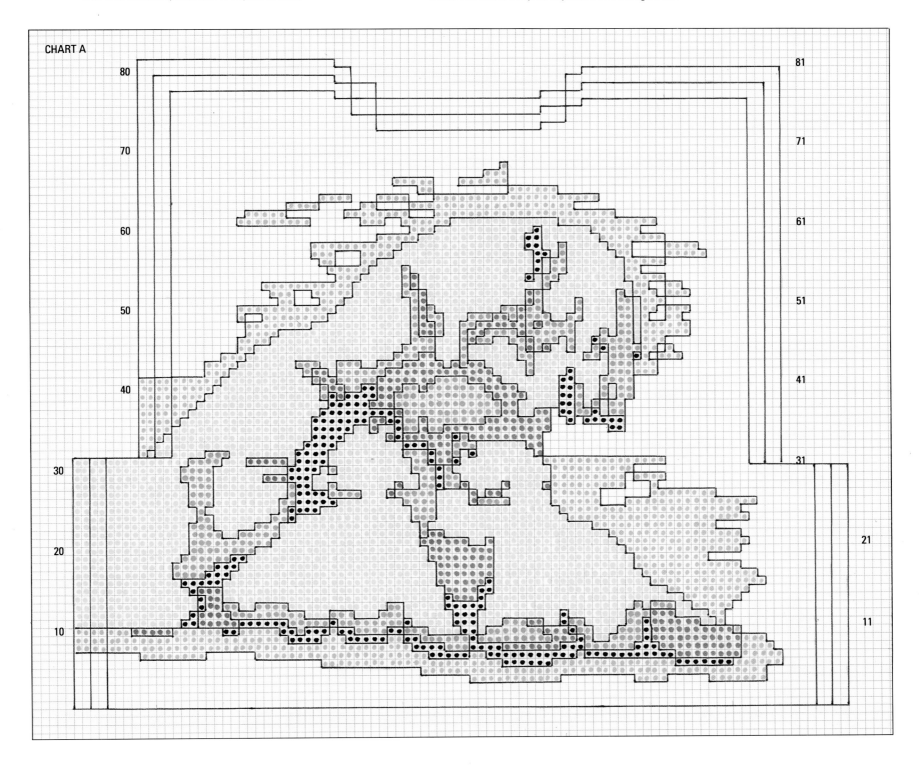

CHART A

POLAR BEARS

CHART C

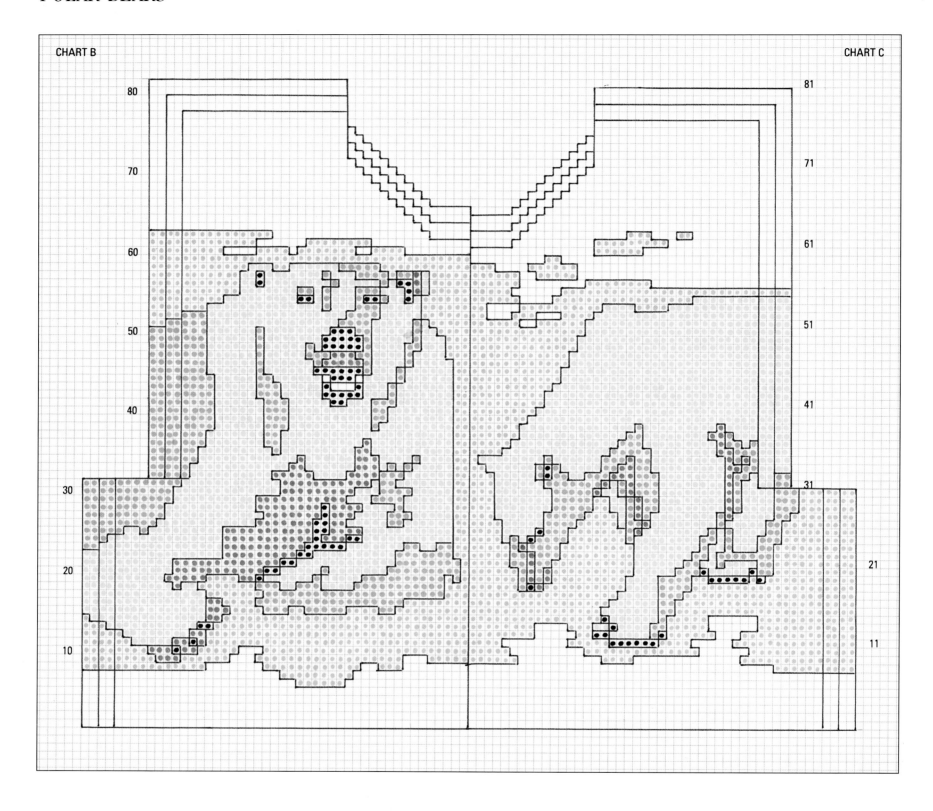

CHART D

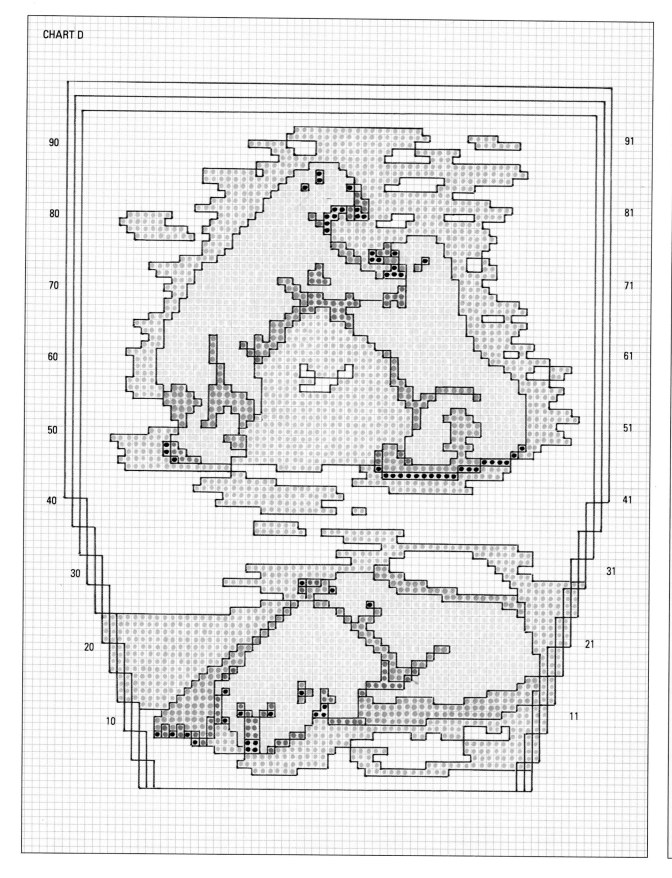

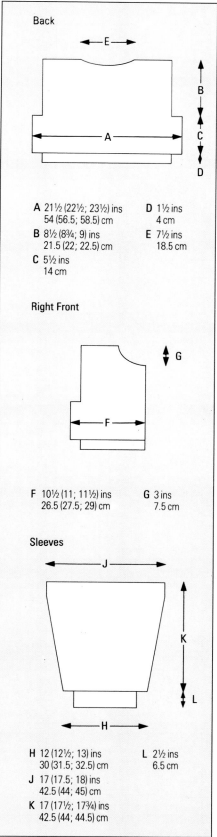

Back

A 21½ (22½; 23½) ins
54 (56.5; 58.5) cm

B 8½ (8¾; 9) ins
21.5 (22; 22.5) cm

C 5½ ins
14 cm

D 1½ ins
4 cm

E 7½ ins
18.5 cm

Right Front

F 10½ (11; 11½) ins
26.5 (27.5; 29) cm

G 3 ins
7.5 cm

Sleeves

H 12 (12½; 13) ins
30 (31.5; 32.5) cm

J 17 (17.5; 18) ins
42.5 (44; 45) cm

K 17 (17½; 17¾) ins
42.5 (44; 44.5) cm

L 2½ ins
6.5 cm

POLAR BEARS

Shape front neck

Next row: P. to last 7 sts., p.2 tog., turn and leave rem. 5 sts. on a holder.

Work on these sts. only.

** Dec. 1 st. at neck edge only on every row until 20 (22, 24) sts. remain.

Work 5 rows straight. Cast off. **

LEFT FRONT

Using 4mm needles and blanc, cast on 49 (51, 53) sts.

Work 8 rows in rib as given for back, inc. 1 st. at end of last row: 50 (52, 54) sts.

Change to 4½mm needles and k. to last 7 sts., turn and leave rem. 7 sts. on a holder.

Work on these sts. only from row 2 of Chart C, shaping armhole as given for back at beg. of row 31: 42 (44, 46) sts.

Cont. until row 60 has been completed.

Shape left front neck

Next row: K. to last 5 sts., turn and leave rem. 5 sts. on a holder.

Work on these sts. only.

Work as given for right front from ** to **.

SLEEVES

Using 4mm needles and blanc, cast on 37 (39, 41) sts.

Work in rib as given for back for 6.5cm ending rib row 1.

Inc. row: Rib 3 (5, 5), m.1, * rib 3, m.1, rep. from * to last 4 (4, 6) sts., rib to end: 48 (50, 52) sts.

Change to 4½mm needles and work from row 1 of Chart D.

Shape sleeves by inc. 1 st. each end of 5th and every foll. 4th row until there are 68 (70, 72) sts.

Work straight until row 94 (96, 98) has been completed from Chart D. Cast off.

BUTTONBAND

Return to 7 sts. on stitch holder on left front.

Using 4mm needles and blanc, with RS facing, join yarn to first st. and work 60 (62, 64) rows rib as set.

Leave these sts. on a stitch holder.

Stitch buttonband to left front matching row by row.

BUTTONHOLE BAND

Return to 7 sts. on holder on right front. Using 4mm needles and blanc, with WS facing, join yarn to first st.

** Work in rib as set until 18 rows have been worked from last buttonhole, then work 2 rows for buttonhole **.

Work from ** to ** twice more (4 buttonholes made).

Work 4 rows rib, leave these sts. on stitch holder.

Stitch buttonhole band to right front, matching row by row.

COLLAR

Join shoulder seams.

Using 4mm needles and blanc, with RS facing and starting at right front, rib across 7 sts. from buttonhole band as set, k. across 5 sts. from holder, pick up and k.19 sts. up right front neck, 11 sts. down right back neck, k. across 20 sts. from holder, pick up and k.12 sts. up left back neck, 19 sts. down left front, k. across 5 sts. from stitch holder and rib 7 sts. from buttonband as set: 105 sts.

Row 1: Rib 7, p. to last 7 sts., rib 7.

Starting rib row 1 as given for back, work 6 (4, 2) rows rib.

Dec. row: Rib 8, k.3 tog., rib to last 11 sts., sl.1, k.2 tog., psso, rib 8: 101 sts.

Starting rib row 2 as given for back, work 5 rows rib.

Buttonhole row: Rib 2, cast off 2 sts., rib 3, k.3 tog., rib to last 11 sts., sl.1, k.2 tog., psso, rib 8.

Next row: Rib to buttonhole, cast on 2 sts., rib to end: 97 sts.

Starting rib row 1 as given for back, rib 3 (5, 7) rows.

Cast off.

TO MAKE UP

Block and press pieces lightly under a damp cloth foll. ball band instructions. Joining cast off edge of armhole to underarms, sew in sleeves, then join side and sleeve seams. Sew on buttons. Sew press stud at top of front opening.

BABY SEALS

SIZES

To fit 46 (48, 51, 56)cm – 18 (19, 20, 22)in chest

Age 0–6 (6–12; 12–18; 24) months

MATERIALS

Patons Beehive Soft Blend DK

Sweater

2 (3, 3, 4) × 50g balls Cornflower (shade 6977)

1 × 50g balls each of White (shade 6963), Grey (6984),
Black (6955) and Silver Grey (6962)

Leggings

2 × 50g balls White (shade 6963)

1 × 50g balls each of Cornflower (shade 6977), Grey
(6984)

A pair each of 3mm (No. 11) and 3½mm (No. 9) knitting
needles

3 × 1cm (½ in) buttons

Round elastic to fit waist

TENSION

24 sts. and 31 rows to 10cm over patt. worked on 3½mm
needles

Check your tension

NOTES

Instructions for larger sizes are given in brackets ( ).
When working motif, use separate, small balls of yarn.
When joining in a new colour, leave an end of about 5cm
for darning in later, and when changing colour, twist yarns
together at back of work to avoid making a hole.

BACK

** Using 3mm needles and cornflower, cast on 60 (62, 64,
72) sts.

Rib row: *K.1, p.1; rep. from * to end.

Rep rib row for 3.5cm ending with RS row.

Inc. row: Rib 7 (9, 9, 5), m.1, * rib 9, m.1; rep. from * to last
8 (8, 10, 4) sts., rib. to end: 66 (68, 70, 80) sts. **

Change to 3½mm needles and work 6 (8, 10, 16) rows
st.st.

'Baby Seals' modelled by
Harry Rutherford, new-born
of Angie Rutherford.

Next row: K.13 (14, 15, 20) sts., work row 1 from Chart A,
k.14 (15, 16, 21) sts.

Cont. without shaping until row 74 has been completed
from Chart.

3rd and 4th sizes only:

Using cornflower, work 4 (8) rows st.st.

All sizes

Shape back neck

Next row: K.26 (27, 27, 32) sts., turn and leave rem. sts. on
a holder.

Crisp, blue colour
provides a perfect
backdrop for these cute Seal
cubs. Reproduced in
beautiful detail, the softness
is created with grey hues. A
simple snowflake jacquard on
the back and sleeves and
three-button neck opening
complete the design.

BABY SEALS

Work on these sts. only.

Next row: Cast off 4 sts., p. to end.

K.1 row.

Next row: Cast off 2 sts., p. to end.

Cast off.

With RS facing, slip first 14 (14, 16, 16) sts. onto a holder.

Rejoin yarn and K. to end.

Work 2nd side of back neck to match first side, reversing all shaping.

Cast off.

FRONT

Work as given for back from ** to **. Change to 3½mm needles and work 17 (19, 25, 31) rows st.st.

Now work rows 1–45 (45, 47, 49) from Chart B (note: row 1 is a p. row).

Shape front neck

Next row: Working in patt., k.27 (28, 29, 34) sts., turn and leave rem. sts. on a holder.

Work on these sts. only.

Cornflower (6977)
White (6963)
Grey (6984)
Silver Grey (6962)
Black (6955)

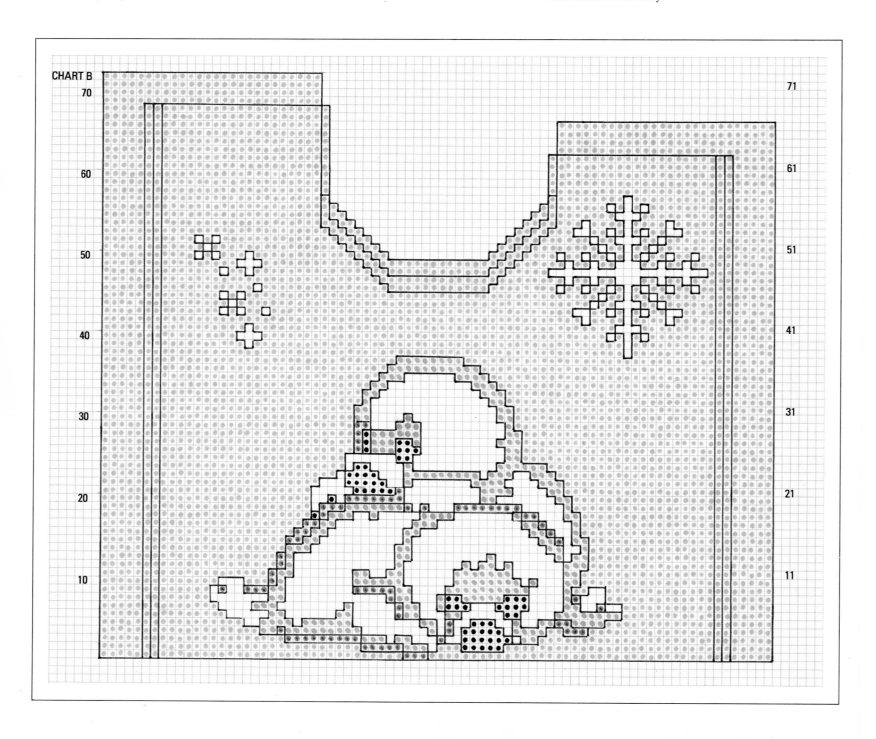

Dec. 1 st. at neck edge only on every row until 19 (20, 22, 26) sts. rem.

Work 8 (8, 7, 8) rows straight.

Cast off.

With RS facing, slip first 12 sts. onto a holder, rejoin yarn and k. to end.

Dec. 1 st. at neck edge only on every row until 19 (20, 22, 26) sts. rem.

Work 14 (14, 13,14) rows straight.

Cast off.

SLEEVES

Using 3mm needles and cornflower, cast on 36 (36, 38, 40) sts.

Rep. rib row as given for back for 3cm ending with RS row.

Inc. row: Rib 5 (5, 6, 7), m.1, * rib 3, m.1; rep. from * to last 4 (4, 5, 6) sts., rib to end: 46 (46, 48, 50) sts.

Change to 3½mm needles and work from row 19 (1, 1, 1) of Chart C. Shape sides by inc. 1 st. at each end of 7th, then

every foll. 6th row until there are 54 (58, 62, 56) sts, then every foll. 4th row until there are 60 (64, 68, 74) sts.

Work 3 rows straight.

Cast off.

NECKBAND

Join right shoulder seam.

Using 3mm needles and cornflower, with RS facing, pick up and k.16 (16, 17, 17) sts. down left front neck, k. across 12 sts. from holder, pick up and k.22 (22, 23, 23) sts. up right front neck, pick up and k.8 sts. down right back neck, k. across 14 (14, 16, 16) sts. from holder, pick up and k.9 sts. up left back neck: 81 (81, 85, 85) sts.

P.1 row.

Rib row 1: K.1, * p.1, k.1; rep. from * to end.

Rib row 2: P.1 * k.1, p.1; rep. from * to end.

Rep. 2 rib rows twice more.

Cast off in rib.

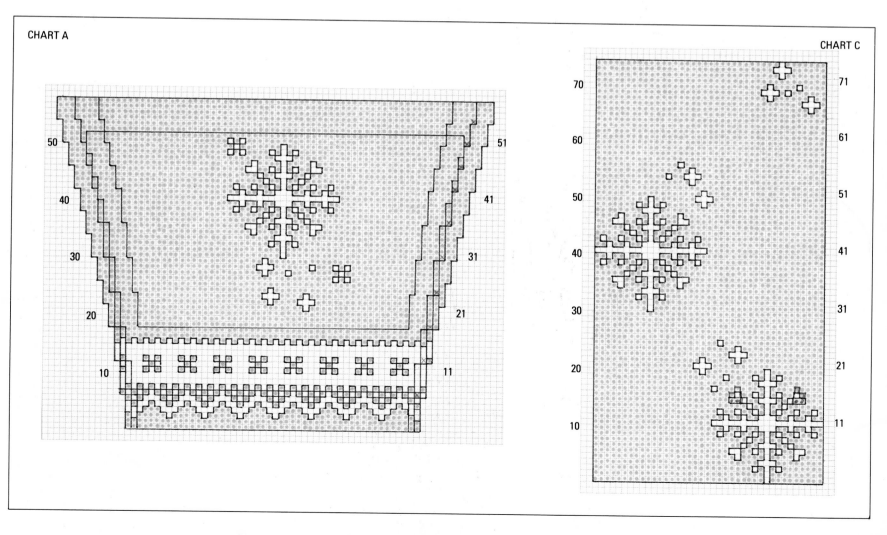

BUTTONBAND

With RS facing, using 3mm needles and cornflower, pick up and k.29 (31, 31, 37) sts. across neckband and left back shoulder. P.1 row.

Rep. 2 rib rows as given for neckband 3 times.

Cast off in rib.

BUTTONHOLE BAND

With RS facing, using 3mm needles and cornflower, pick up and k.29 (31, 31, 37) sts. across left front shoulder and neckband edge. P.1 row.

Rep. 2 rib rows as given for neckband, once.

Next row: Rib 3, * yfwd, rib 2 tog., rib 9 (10, 10, 11); rep. from * once, yfwd, rib 2 tog., rib 2 (2, 2, 6).

Starting with rib row 2, work 3 rows in k.1, p.1 rib as given for neckband.

Cast off in rib.

TO MAKE UP

Lap buttonhole band over buttonband and stitch together at armhole edge. Block and press pieces lightly under a damp cloth following ball band instructions. Sew in sleeves. Join side and sleeve seams. Sew on buttons to correspond with buttonholes.

LEGGINGS (Make 2)

Using 3½mm needles and cornflower, cast on 64 (68, 72, 86) sts.

Work in k.1, p.1 rib as given for sweater back in the foll. colours: 2 rows cornflower, 2 rows white, 2 rows grey, 2 rows white.

Rep. 8 row stripe patt. throughout and at the same time, inc. 1 st. at each end of every 2nd (4th, 4th, 4th) row 20 (5, 11, 19) times, then every foll. alt row 4 (19, 13, 5) times, taking new sts. into rib: 112 (116, 120, 134) sts.

Cont. until work measures 18 (21, 25, 30)cm. from beg.

Shape top of leg

Cast off 3 sts. at beg. of next 2 rows, 2 sts. at beg. of foll. 2 rows, then 1 st. at each end of next row: 100 (104, 108, 122) sts. Cont. straight until work measures 32.5 (37, 42, 47) cm, ending with 2nd row white.

Shape waist

(Work short rows)

1st row: Rib 66 (69, 72, 81) sts., yfwd, sl.1, turn.

2nd row: yfwd, sl.1, ybk, rib to end.

3rd row: Rib 44 (46, 48, 54) sts., yfwd, sl.1, turn.

4th row: as 2nd.

5th row: Rib 22, (23, 24, 27) sts., yfwd, sl.1, turn.

6th row: as 2nd.

Now work 2 rows white across all sts.

Change to 3mm needles and using cornflower, work 4 cm in k.1, p.1 rib.

Cast off in rib.

TO MAKE UP

Turn one leg to wrong side in order to match short row stripes at centre back. Join centre back and front seams. Join leg seams, reversing seam for last 3cm for ankle cuff. Thread elastic through waistband.

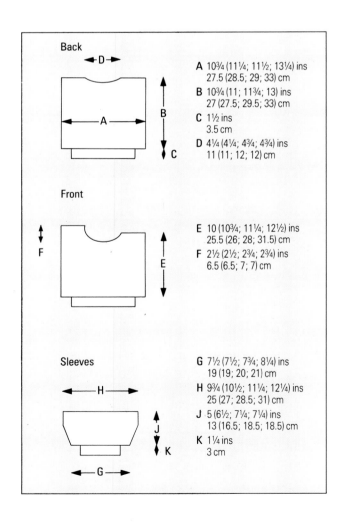

Back

←D→

A 10¾ (11¼; 11½; 13¼) ins
27.5 (28.5; 29; 33) cm

B 10¾ (11; 11¾; 13) ins
27 (27.5; 29.5; 33) cm

C 1½ ins
3.5 cm

D 4¼ (4¼; 4¾; 4¾) ins
11 (11; 12; 12) cm

Front

E 10 (10¾; 11¼; 12½) ins
25.5 (26; 28; 31.5) cm

F 2½ (2½; 2¾; 2¾) ins
6.5 (6.5; 7; 7) cm

Sleeves

←H→

G 7½ (7½; 7¾; 8¼) ins
19 (19; 20; 21) cm

H 9¾ (10½; 11¼; 12¼) ins
25 (27; 28.5; 31) cm

J 5 (6½; 7¼; 7¼) ins
13 (16.5; 18.5; 18.5) cm

K 1¼ ins
3 cm

←G→

Much loved by people throughout the world, Elephants are coming under increasing threat in their natural habitat. Between 30,000 and 40,000 of the rarer Asian Elephant currently survive in the forests of South and South-east Asia, although this number is constantly decreasing as these forests are logged or cleared for agriculture. The only places where Asian Elephants are at all secure are a few large national parks such as Taman Negara in Malaysia. By far the biggest threat to the African Elephant is poaching for ivory. Despite legal protection in many countries and international controls on ivory trade, tens of thousands of Elephants are killed each year and the ivory smuggled abroad. The overall population has dropped from an estimated 1,250,000 in the late 1970s to fewer than 750,000 today. Fortunately some countries, most notably Zimbabwe, are working hard to conserve their Elephant populations.

African ELEPHANTS *Mother and Calf*

SIZES

To fit 67.5 (75, 79, 83)cm – 27 (30, 32, 33)in chest
Age 7 (9, 11, 13) years.

MATERIALS

Pingouin France + DK
2 (2, 3, 3) × 50g balls Persan (shade 13)
2 × 50g balls Turquoise (shade 14)
2 (2, 3, 3) × 50g balls Soleil (shade 10)
1 × 50g balls each of Souris (shade 19),
Blanc (01), Perle (18) and Noir (20)
A pair each of 3mm (No. 11) and 3¾mm (No. 9) knitting needles
Stitch holder

TENSION

24 sts. and 28 rows to 10cm over patt. worked on 3¾mm needles
Check your tension

NOTES

Instructions for larger sizes are given in brackets ( ).
When working motif, use separate, small balls of yarn.
When joining in a new colour, leave an end of about 5cm for darning in later. When changing colour, twist yarns together at back of work to avoid making a hole.

BACK

** Using 3mm needles and persan, cast on 90 (96, 100, 104) sts.
Rib row: * K.1, p.1; rep. from * to end.
Rep. rib row for 6cm, ending with RS row.
Inc. row: Rib 10 (13, 15, 17), m.1, * rib 14, m.1; rep. from * to last 10 (13, 15, 17) sts., rib to end: 96 (102, 106, 110) sts.
Change to 3¾mm needles and work 21 (25, 29, 35) rows st.st. **
Work rows 1–41 from Chart A (Note: row 1 is a p. row).

Shape armholes

Cast off 4 (5, 6,6) sts. at beg. of next 2 rows: 88 (92, 94, 98) sts. Cont. working straight until row 85 (87, 91, 93) has been completed.

Shape back neck

Next row: K.32 (33, 33, 34), turn and leave rem. sts. on a spare needle.
Work on these sts. only.
Next row: Cast off 5 sts., p. to end.

K.1 row.

Next row: Cast off 4 sts., p. to end.

Cast off.

Return to rem. sts.

With RS facing, slip first 24 (26, 28, 30) sts. onto a stitch holder.

Rejoin yarn to first st. and k. to end.

Complete 2nd side of back neck to match first, reversing all shaping.

FRONT

Work as given for back from ** to **, then work rows 1–41 from Chart B (note: row 1 is a p. row).

Shape armholes

Cast off 4 (5, 6, 6) sts. at beg. of next 2 rows: 88 (92, 94, 98) sts.

Cont. working straight until row 75 (77, 81, 83) has been completed.

Shape front neck

Next row: K.32 (33, 33, 34) sts., turn and leave rem. sts. on a stitch holder.

Work on these sts. only.

Dec. 1 st. at neck edge only on every row until 23 (24, 24, 25) sts. rem.

Work 4 rows straight. Cast off.

Return to rem. sts.

With RS facing, slip first 24 (26, 28, 30) sts. onto a holder.

Rejoin yarn to first st. and k. to end.

Complete 2nd side of front neck to match first, reversing all shaping.

SLEEVES

** Using 3mm needles and turquoise, cast on 45 (49, 51, 55) sts. Work 6cm of k.1, p.1 rib, ending with a RS row.

Inc. row: Rib 1 (3, 1, 3), m.1, * rib 3, m.1; rep. from * to last 2 (4, 2, 4) sts., rib to end: 60 (64, 68, 72) sts.

Change to 3¾mm needles and work from row 13 (7, 3, 1) Chart C for left sleeve or Chart D for right sleeve, at the same time, shape sleeve by inc. 1 st. at each end of 5th and every foll. 6th row until there are 82 (86, 92, 96) sts.

Work straight until row 96 (96, 98, 100) of chart has been completed.

Cast off.

'African Elephants'
modelled by Kate Rutherford,
eldest and only daughter
of the Rutherford Brood.

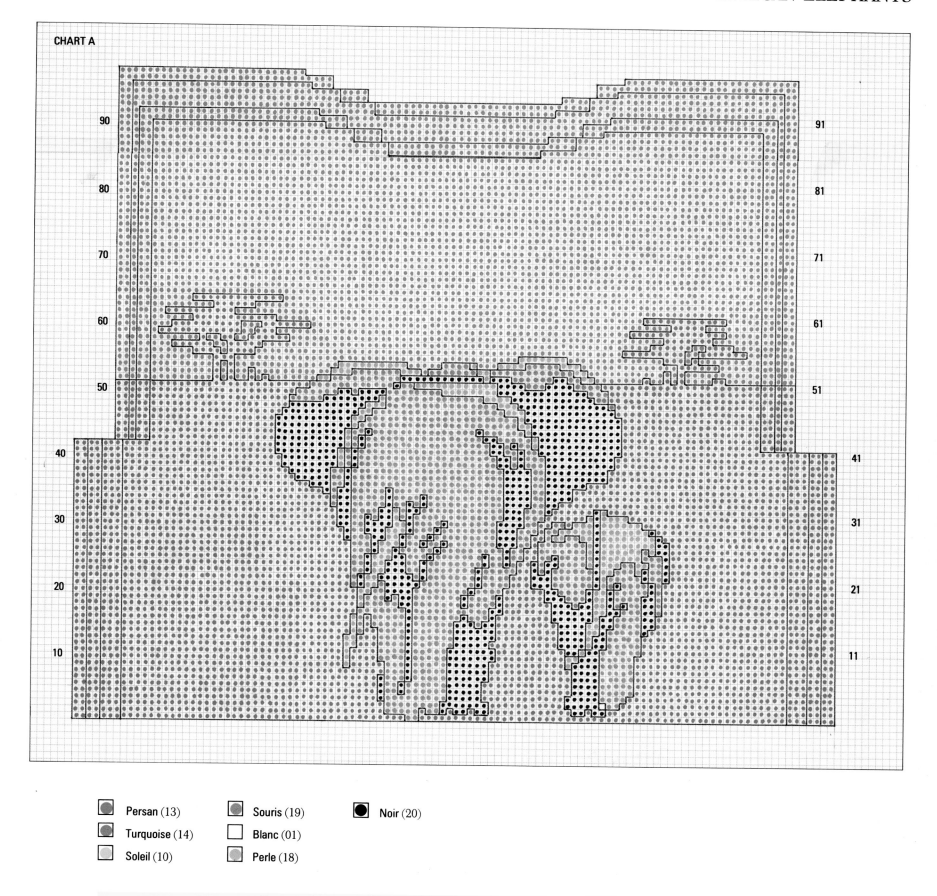

CHART A

Persan (13)   Souris (19)   Noir (20)

Turquoise (14)   Blanc (01)

Soleil (10)   Perle (18)

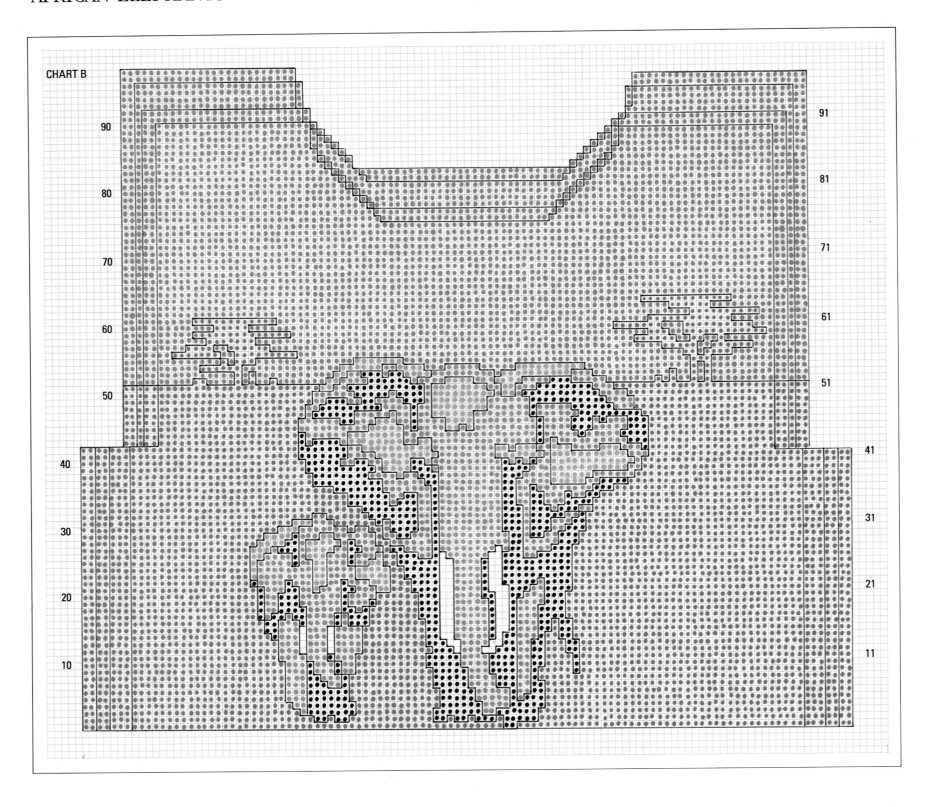

CHART B

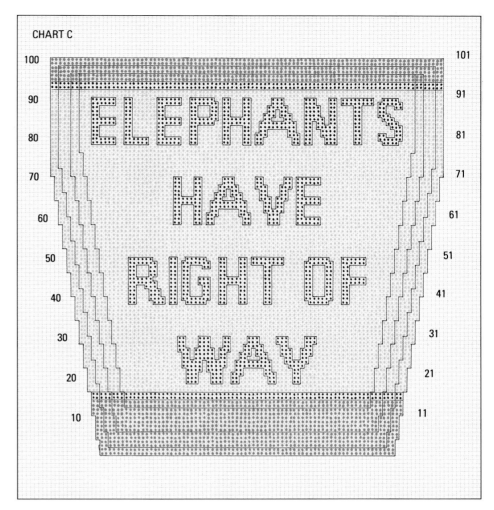

CHART C

NECKBAND

Join left shoulder.

Using 3mm needles and turquoise and with RS facing, pick up and k.13 sts. down right back neck, k. across 24 (26, 28, 30) sts. from holder, pick up and k.14 sts. up left back neck, 16 sts. down left front neck, k. across 12 (13, 14, 15) sts. from holder, place centre front marker, k. across 12 (13, 14, 15) sts. from holder, then pick up and k.16 sts. up right front neck: 107 (111, 115, 119) sts.

P.1 row.

Work 5 rows in k.1, p.1 rib.

Cast off in rib.

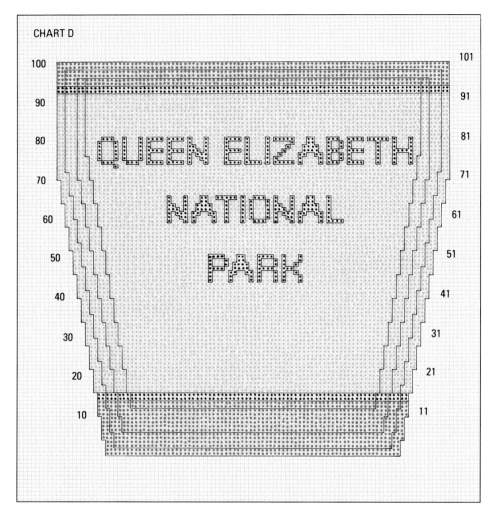

CHART D

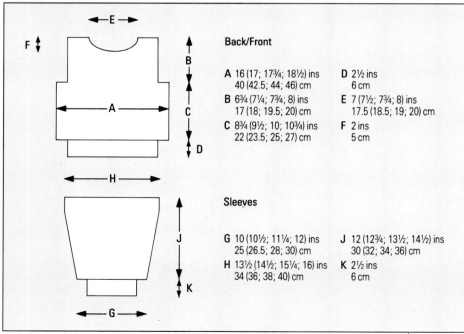

← E →

F ↕

Back/Front

A 16 (17; 17¾; 18½) ins
40 (42.5; 44; 46) cm

B 6¾ (7¼; 7¾; 8) ins
17 (18; 19.5; 20) cm

C 8¾ (9½; 10; 10¾) ins
22 (23.5; 25; 27) cm

D 2½ ins
6 cm

E 7 (7½; 7¾; 8) ins
17.5 (18.5; 19; 20) cm

F 2 ins
5 cm

Sleeves

G 10 (10½; 11¼; 12) ins
25 (26.5; 28; 30) cm

H 13½ (14½; 15¼; 16) ins
34 (36; 38; 40) cm

J 12 (12¾; 13½; 14½) ins
30 (32; 34; 36) cm

K 2½ ins
6 cm

COLLAR

Using 3mm needles and noir, cast on 107 (111, 115, 119) sts.

Working in k.1, p.1 rib, work 1 row noir, 22 rows soleil, 1 row turquoise. Using turquoise, cast off in rib.

TO MAKE UP

Block and press pieces lightly under a damp cloth following ball band instructions. Join right shoulder and neckband seam. Starting at centre front marker, stitch cast-off edge of collar to inside edge of neckband base, stitch by stitch. Join edges of collar at centre front for 1.5cm. Joining cast-off edge of armhole to underarms, sew in sleeves, then join side and sleeve seams.

Looking like a relic from a prehistoric era, the Black Rhinoceros is in grave danger of following the mammoths and dinosaurs into the history books. Twenty years ago there were around 70,000 of them, in central, eastern and southern Africa. Now there are fewer than 3,000 and the number is dropping fast. The sole reason for this is the Rhino's horn, which can command high prices both in the Yemen Arab Republic, where it is used to make much sought-after dagger handles, and in the Far East where it is used in traditional medicines for treating fevers. Groups of heavily armed poachers have swept through Africa wiping out entire Rhino populations in their pursuit of the horn, often fighting pitch battles with wildlife guards and rangers in the process. The only hope of saving the last few viable populations, such as the one in the Zambezi valley in Zimbabwe, is to put a complete halt to the trade in the horn.

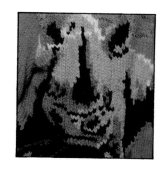

Black RHINO

SIZES
One size to fit 80–100cm – 32–40in chest

MATERIALS
Pingouin Chunky
13 × 50g balls Beige (shade 11)
2 × 50g balls Noir (shade 16)
1 × 50g balls each of Blanc (shade 01), Nuage (12), Souris (17)
Pingouin Mohican, flecked chunky
4 × 50g balls Souris (shade 11)
Pingouin Sweet' hair
1 × 50g ball Prune (shade 14)
A pair each of 5mm (No. 6) and 6mm (No. 4) needles
Stitch holder

TENSION
14 sts. and 16 rows to 10cm over patt. worked on 6mm needles
Check your tension

NOTES
When working motif, use separate small balls of yarn.
When joining in a new colour, leave an end of about 5cm for darning in later. When changing colour, twist yarns together at back of work to avoid making a hole.

BACK
** Using 5mm needles and beige, cast on 69 sts.
Rib row 1: K.1, * p.1, k.1; rep. from * to end.
Rib row 2: P.1, * k.1, p.1; rep. from * to end.
Rep. these 2 rows for 9cm ending with rib row 1.
Inc. row: Rib 5, m.1, * rib 6, m.1; rep. from * to last 4 sts., rib 4: 80 sts. **
Change to 6mm needles and work 22 rows st.st.
Now work rows 1–7 from Chart A, placing chart after first 23 sts. Work 4 rows st.st., then work rows 1–7 from Chart B, placing chart after first 25 sts. Work 16 rows st.st.

Shape raglans
Cast off 2 sts. at beg. of next 2 rows, then dec. 1 st. at each end of next row: 74 sts.
P.1 row, then work rows 1–12 from Chart C, dec. 1 st. at each end of rows 1, 3, 5, 8 and 11, placing first row of chart after first 15 sts: 64 sts.
Work 6 rows st.st., dec. 1 st. at each end of 2nd and 5th rows: 60 sts.
Change to souris (Shade 11) and work rows 1–12 from

Standing strong and powerful, the distinctive shapes of the Black Rhinos are worked in intarsia knitting. Simple embroidery added in a contrast yarn represents sun-scorched grass. Chunky yarn is used and the look is completed with garter stitch shoulders and a tight roll-neck.

Chart D, dec. 1 st. at each end of rows 2, 5,8, and 11, placing first row of chart after first 9 sts.; 52 sts.

Using souris (Shade 11), p.1 row, then dec. 1 st. at each end of every row until 30 sts. rem.

Shape back neck

Next row: K.2 tog., k.9, turn and leave rem. sts. on a spare needle. Work on these 10 sts. only.

Cont. dec. 1 st. at raglan edge on every row, at the same time, cast off 3 sts. at beg. of next and foll. alt. row.

Cast off rem. 1 st. Return to sts. on spare needle.

With RS facing, slip first 8 sts. onto a holder, rejoin yarn to first st., k. to last 2 sts., k.2 tog.

Complete 2nd side of back neck to match first side, reversing all shaping.

FRONT

Work as given for back from ** to **.

Change to 6mm needles and work rows 1–92 from Chart E, shaping armholes at row 57 and raglans as indicated on chart: 46 sts.

Shape front neck

Next row: K.2 tog., k.16, turn and leave rem. sts. on a holder.

Work on these sts. only.

Dec. 1 st. at each end of every row until 9 sts. rem.

Then dec. at raglan edge only on every row until 2 sts. rem. Cast off.

Return to sts. on holder.

With RS facing, slip first 10 sts. onto holder, rejoin yarn to first st. and k. to last 2 sts., k.2 tog.

Complete 2nd side of front neck to match first side, reversing all shaping.

'Black Rhino' modelled by accomplished stage and TV actor Paul Nicholas. Originally a singer, he has starred in many West End musicals, including, Hair, Mutiny on the Bounty *and* Cats. *He has been involved with the WWF on previous occasions.*

SLEEVES

Using 5mm needles and beige, cast on 31 sts.

Rep. 2 rib rows as given for back for 7.5cm, ending with rib row 1.

Inc. row: Rib 1, m.1, * rib 3, m.1; rep. from * to end: 42 sts.

Change to 6mm needles and proceed in st.st., inc. 1 st. at each end of 5th and every foll. 6th row until there are 60 sts.

Work 15 rows without shaping.

Shape raglans

Cast off 2 sts. at beg. of next 2 rows, then dec. 1 st. at each end of every row until 28 sts. rem.

Change to souris (11) and proceed in garter st., dec. 1 st. at each end of next and every foll. alt. row until 18 sts. rem.

Then dec. 1 st. at each end of every foll. 4th row until 8 sts. rem. P.1 row.

Right sleeve only

Cast off 3 sts. at beg. of next and foll. alt. row. P.1 row. Cast off rem. 2 sts.

Left sleeve only

K.1 row. Cast off 3 sts. at beg. of next and foll. alt. row. Cast off rem. 2 sts.

- ⬤ Beige (11)
- ⬤ Noir (16)
- ⬤ Souris (11)
- ☐ Blanc (01)
- ⬤ Nuage (12)
- ⬤ Souris (17)

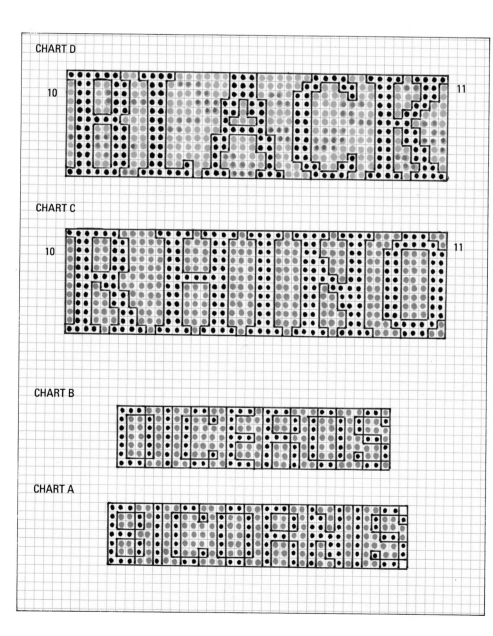

BLACK RHINO

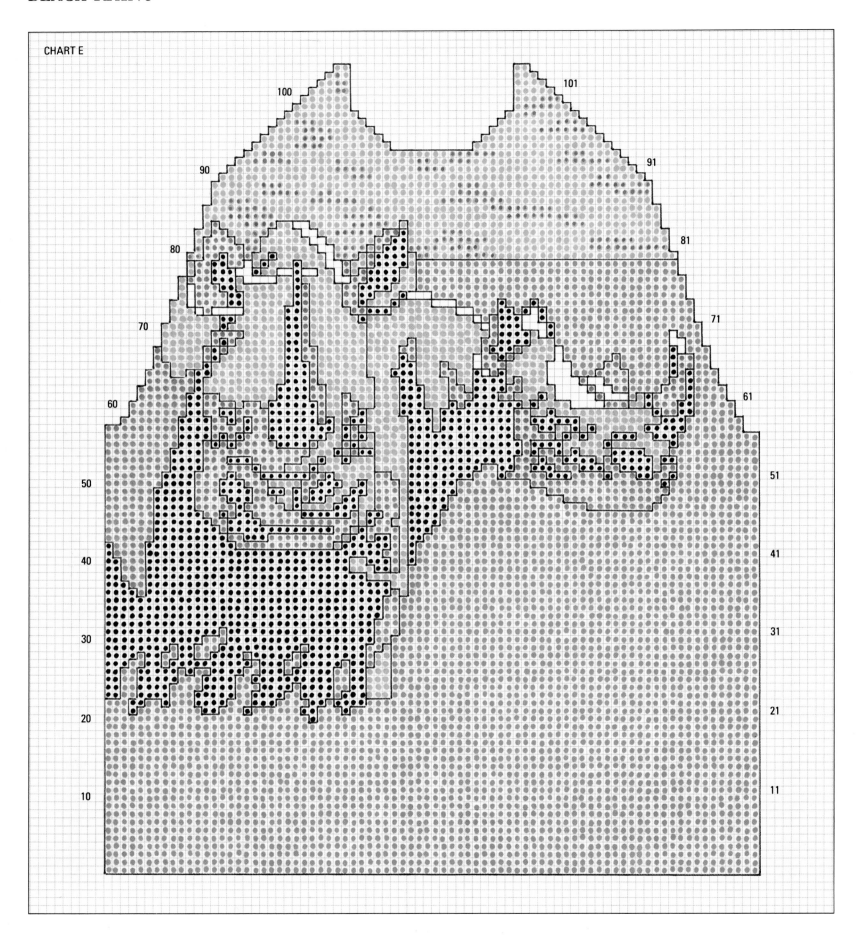

NECKBAND

Join both front and the left back raglan seams.

Using 5mm needles and souris (11), with RS facing, pick up and k.11 sts. down right back neck, k.8 sts. from holder, pick up and k.12 sts. up left back neck, 8 sts. across left sleeve, 14 sts. down left front neck, k.10 sts. from holder, pick up and k.14 sts. up right front neck, 8 sts. across right sleeve: 85 sts. P.1 row.

Cast off.

COLLAR

Using 5mm needles and souris (11), cast on 85 sts.

Rep. 2 rib rows as given for back for 16 rows.

Cast off in rib.

TO MAKE UP

Block and press pieces lightly under a damp cloth foll. ball band instructions. With WS tog., backstitch cast-off edge of collar to neckband, stitch by stitch. Join right raglan and collar seam. Join side and underarm seams. Using Sweet' hair embroider 'grass' in backstitch as shown on Chart E.

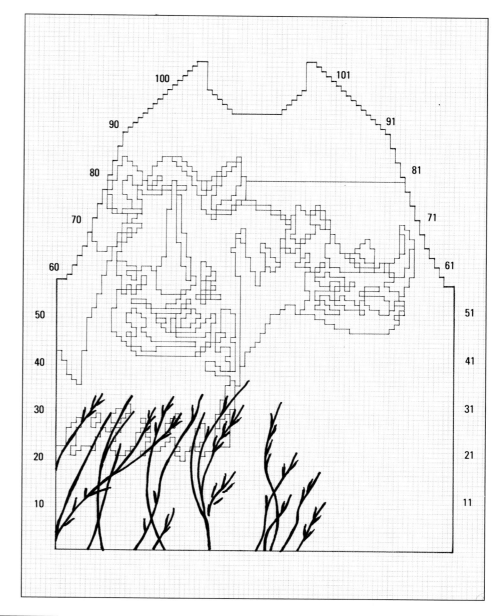

◻ Backstitch embroidery using prune (14)

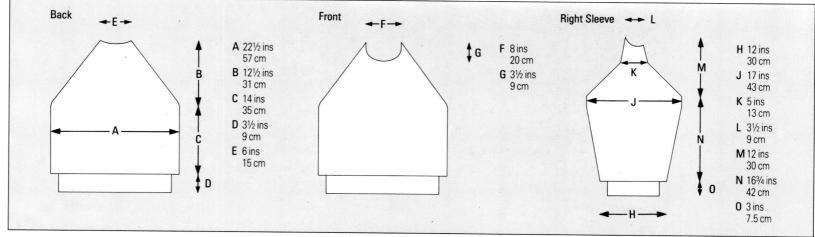

Back   ←E→

A 22½ ins 57 cm
B 12½ ins 31 cm
C 14 ins 35 cm
D 3½ ins 9 cm
E 6 ins 15 cm

Front   ←F→

F 8 ins 20 cm
G 3½ ins 9 cm

Right Sleeve ←→ L

H 12 ins 30 cm
J 17 ins 43 cm
K 5 ins 13 cm
L 3½ ins 9 cm
M 12 ins 30 cm
N 16¾ ins 42 cm
O 3 ins 7.5 cm

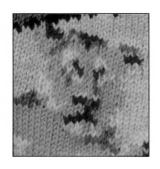

Symbols of might, Lions are still found in many parts of Africa. In the last hundred years they have been exterminated in both the far north of their range, in the Atlas Mountains of Morocco and Algeria, and the far south, in Cape Province in South Africa. Lions were also once found in the Middle East, India and even in southern Europe. The last Lions in Europe were exterminated around 2,000 years ago although in the Middle East they survived well into the nineteenth century. Today, however, the only wild Lions outside Africa live in the Gir Forest in north-east India where around 150 are closely protected in a wildlife sanctuary. Many African Lions are also protected in national parks and game reserves, where they are immensely popular tourist attractions, but outside these areas they are often killed for preying on domestic livestock and the population as a whole is probably decreasing.

LIONESSES
Sleeping in Acacia tree

▶ A languorous mood is captured in this three-dimensional design. The dead acacia is twisted and knotted; the Lionesses take advantage of the sculptured limbs for slumber. A section of the main garment is translated into a junior version.

SIZES
Adult: One size to fit 80–100cm – 32–40in chest
Child: To fit 62.5 (67.5, 75, 79, 83) cm – 25 (27, 30, 32, 33) in chest. Age 5 (7, 9, 11, 13) years.

MATERIALS
Emu Superwash DK 100% wool
Adult
11 × 50g balls Grey (shade 3043)
2 × 50g balls Dk. Brown (shade 3011)
1 × 50g balls each of Brown (shade 3009), Med. Brown (3099), Lt. Brown (3098), Dk. Gold (3019), Med. Gold (3012), Lt. Gold (3006)

Child
5 (5, 6, 6, 7) × 50g balls Grey (shade 3043)
1 × 50g balls each of Med. Brown (shade 3099), Dk. Brown (3011), Brown (3009), Lt. Brown (3098), Dk. Gold (3019), Med. Gold (3012), Lt. Gold (3006)
Note: apart from the Grey and Med. Brown yarns, the excess yarn from the adult's sweater is sufficient for the child's sweater.
A pair each of 3¼mm (No. 10) and 4mm (No. 8) knitting needles
Stitch holder

TENSION
22 sts. and 30 rows to 10cm over patt. worked on 4mm needles
Check your tension

NOTES
Instructions for larger sizes are given in brackets ( ).
When working motif, use separate, small balls of yarn.
When joining in a new colour, leave an end of about 5cm for darning in later. When changing colour, twist yarns together at back of work to avoid making a hole.

Adult's Sweater

BACK
** Using 3¼mm needles and grey, cast on 127 sts.
Rib row 1: K.1, * p.1, k.1; rep. from * to end.
Rib row 2: P.1, * k.1, p.1; rep. from * to end.
Rep. these 2 rows for 7.5cm ending with Rib row 1.
Inc. row: Rib 6, m.1, * rib 11, m.1; rep. from * to last 11 sts., rib to end: 138 sts.
Change to 4mm needles and work rows 1–100 from Chart A.

'Lionesses' modelled by internationally acclaimed guitarist Mike Rutherford. He was a founder member of Genesis and Mike and the Mechanics. His son Tom models the child's lioness sweater.

LIONESSES

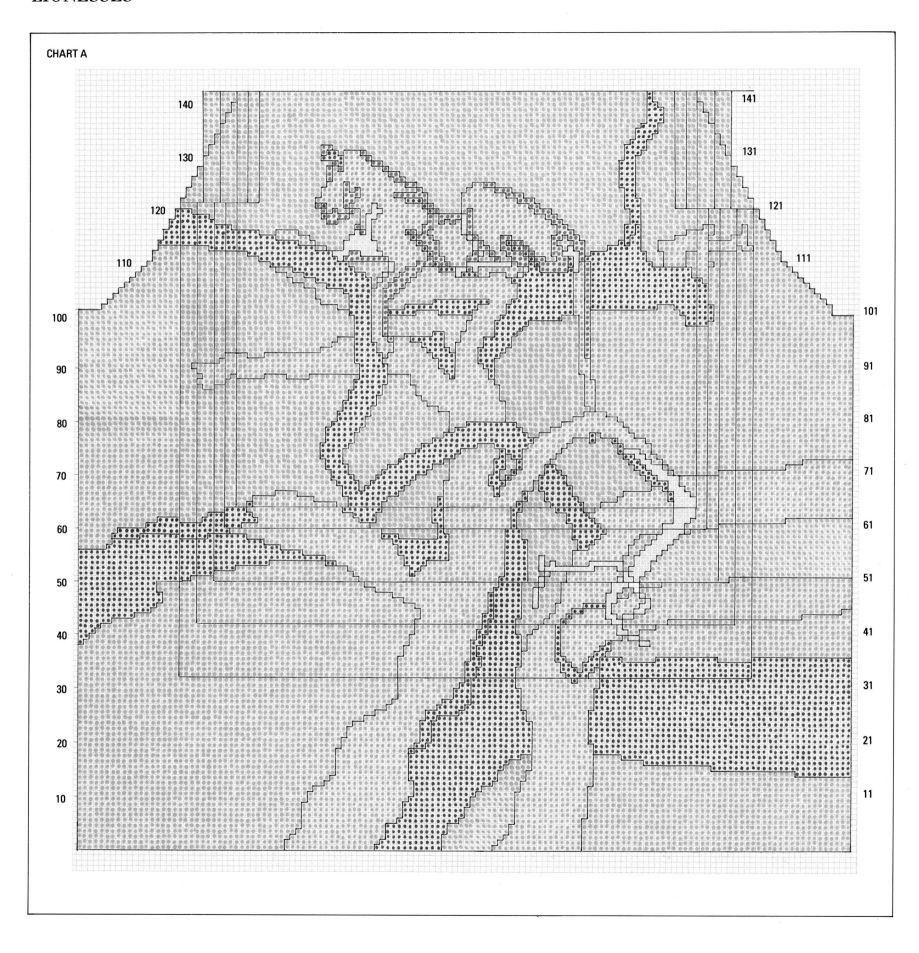

Shape raglans

Working in patt., cast off 4 sts. at beg. of next 2 rows, then dec. 1 st. at each end of foll. 9 rows: 112 sts. **

Now dec. 1 st. at each end of every every alt. row until row 142 from chart has been completed.

Using grey, cont. dec. on every alt. row until 48 sts. remain.

P.1 row.

Shape back neck

Next row: K.2 tog., k.12, turn and leave rem. sts. on a stitch holder.

Next row: Cast off 6 sts., p. to end.

Next row: K.2 tog., k. to end.

Next row: Cast off 5 sts.

Cast off last st.

With RS facing, slip first 20 sts. onto holder.

Rejoin yarn and k. to last 2 sts., k.2 tog.

P.1 row.

Next row: Cast off 6 sts., k. to last 2 sts., k.2 tog.

P. 1 row.

Cast off.

FRONT

Work as given for back from ** to **, but work from Chart B.

Now dec. 1 st. at each end of every foll. alt. row until row 150 has been completed. Using grey, cont. dec. on every alt. row until 64 sts. remain.

P.1 row.

Shape front neck

Next row: K.2 tog., k.20, turn and leave rem. sts. on a holder.

Work on these sts. only.

Cont. shaping raglan as before, at the same time, dec. 1 st. at neck edge on every row until 4 sts. remain.

Now cont. shaping raglan only, until 1 st. remains.

Cast off.

With RS facing, slip first 20 sts. onto a holder.

Rejoin yarn and k. to last 2 sts., k.2 tog.

Now complete 2nd side of neck to match first side, reversing all shaping.

LEFT SLEEVE

** Using 3¼mm needles and grey, cast on 61 sts.

Work the 2 rib rows as given for back for 7.5cm, ending with rib row 1.

Inc. row: * Rib 6, m.1; rep. from * to last 7 sts., rib to end: 70 sts.

Change to 4mm needles and inc. 1 st. at each end of 5th and every foll. 4th row until there are 78 sts., ending with a p. row. **

Now work rows 1–86 from Chart C, inc. 1 st. at each end of 5th and foll. 6th row until there are 96 sts.

Shape raglans

Keeping patt. correct, cast off 4 sts. at beg. of next 2 rows.

Then dec. 1 st. at each end of next and every foll. alt. row.

When row 106 from chart has been completed, using grey, cont. dec. as before until 10 sts. remain.

Next row: Cast off 5 sts., p. to end.

Cast off.

 (3043)
 (3011)
(3009)
(3099)
(3098)
(3019)
(3012)
(3006)

LIONESSES

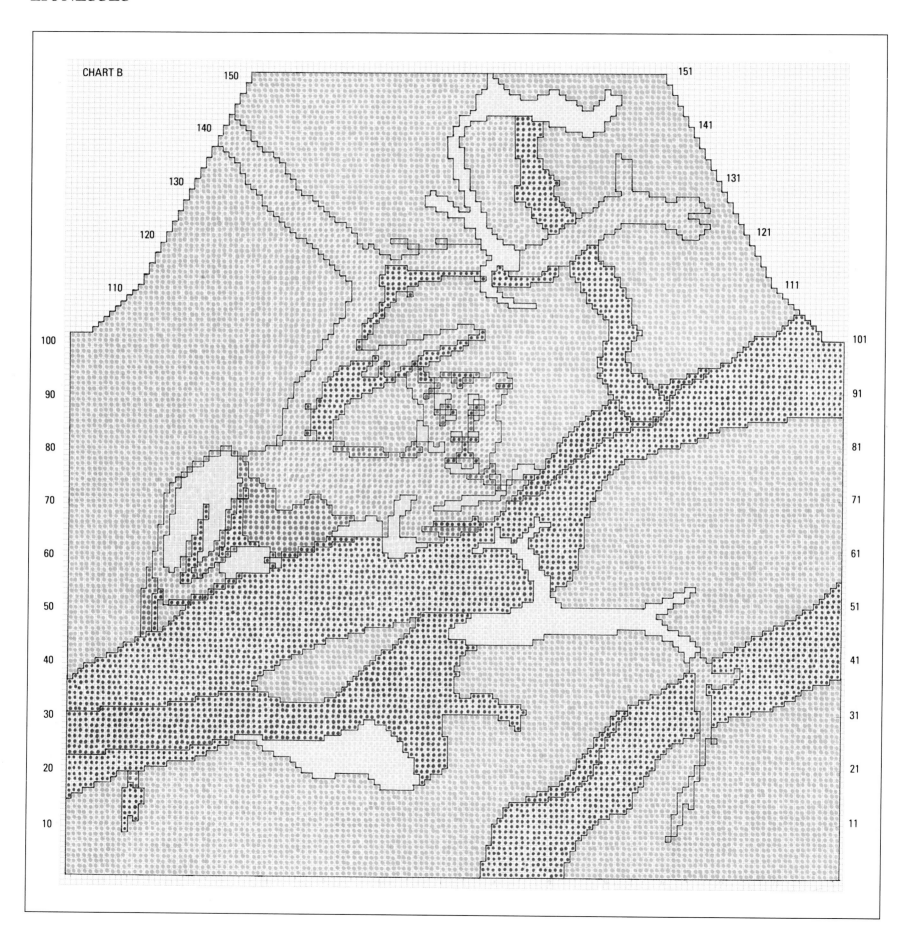

RIGHT SLEEVE

Work as given for left sleeve from ** to **.

Now work rows 1–72 from Chart D, inc. 1 st. at each end of 5th and every foll. 6th row until there are 96 sts.

Using grey, work 14 rows straight.

Shape raglans

Cast off 4 sts. at beg. of next 2 rows. Then dec. 1 st. at each end of next and every foll. alt. row until 54 sts. remain.

Now work rows 1–13 from Chart E.

Using grey, cont. dec. as before until 12 sts. remain.

P.1 row.

Next row: Cast off 6 sts., k. to last 2 sts., k.2 tog.

P.1 row.

Cast off rem. 5 sts.

NECKBAND

Join both front and the left back raglan seams.

With RS facing, using 3¼mm needles and grey, pick up and k.9 sts. down right back neck, k. across 20 sts. from holder, pick up and k.10 sts. up left back neck, 6 sts. across left sleeve, 16 sts. down left front neck, k. across 20 sts. from holder, pick up and k. 16 sts. up right front neck and k. across 6 sts. from right sleeve: 103 sts.

P.1 row.

Then work 10 rows rib as given for back.

Cast off in rib.

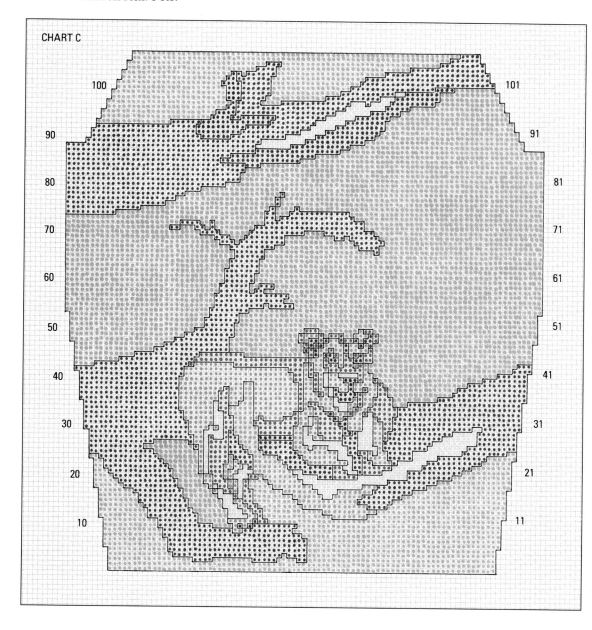

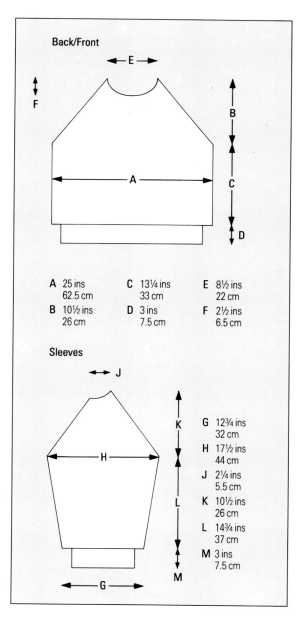

Back/Front

A	25 ins	C	13¼ ins	E	8½ ins
	62.5 cm		33 cm		22 cm
B	10½ ins	D	3 ins	F	2½ ins
	26 cm		7.5 cm		6.5 cm

Sleeves

G	12¾ ins
	32 cm
H	17½ ins
	44 cm
J	2¼ ins
	5.5 cm
K	10½ ins
	26 cm
L	14¾ ins
	37 cm
M	3 ins
	7.5 cm

LIONESSES

COLLAR

Using 3¼mm needles and grey, cast on 103 sts.
Work 32 rows in k.1, p.1 rib as given for back.
Cast off in rib.

TO MAKE UP

Block and press pieces lightly under a damp cloth following ball band instructions. Join right back raglan to neckband seams. Fold neckband in half to WS and slipstitch into position. Starting at centre front, stitch cast-off edge of collar to neckband seam, stitch by stitch. Join side and sleeve seams.

Child's Sweater

BACK

** Using 3¼mm needles and grey, cast on 77 (81, 85, 91, 97) sts.
Work in rib as given for adult's sweater back for 6 cm, ending with rib row 1.
Inc. row: Rib 7 (9, 11, 14, 17), m.1, * rib 16, m.1; rep. from * to last 6 (8, 10, 13, 16) sts., rib to end: 82 (86, 90, 96, 102) sts. **
Change to 4mm needles and work 56 (60, 70, 78, 88) rows st.st.

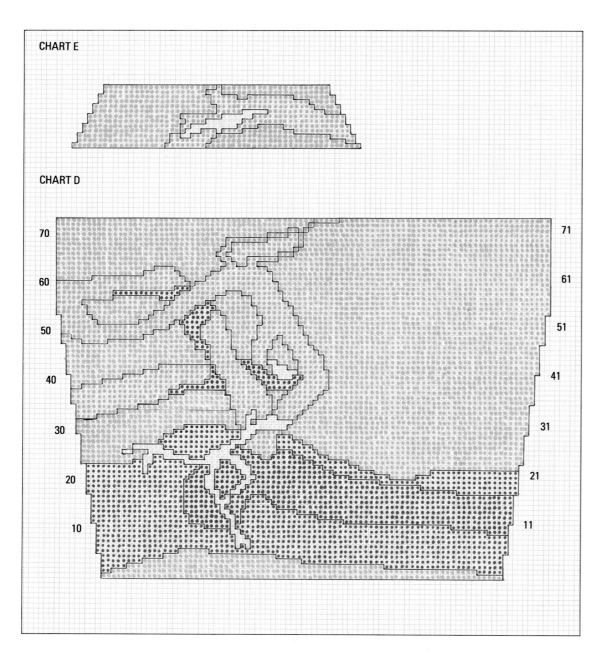

CHART E

CHART D

Shape armholes

Cast off 4 sts. at beg. of next 2 rows: 74 (78, 82, 88, 94) sts.
Work 44 (46, 48, 52, 54) rows straight.

Shape back neck

Next row: K.27 (29, 31, 34, 37) sts., turn and leave rem. sts. on a holder.
Work on these sts only.
Cast off 4 sts., p. to end.
K.1 row.
Cast off 4(4, 4, 4, 5) sts., p. to end.
Cast off rem. 19 (21, 23, 26, 28) sts.
With RS facing , slip first 20 sts. onto a holder. Rejoin yarn and k. to end.
Complete 2nd side of back neck to match first, reversing all shaping.

FRONT

Work as given for back from ** to **.
Change to 4mm needles and starting at row 65 (61, 51, 43, 33) of Chart A, cont. until row 120 has been completed.

Shape armholes

Cast off 4 sts. at beg. of next 2 rows: 74 (78, 82, 88, 94) sts.
Work until row 142 from chart has been completed.
Using grey, work 12 (14, 16, 18, 18) rows straight.

Shape front neck

Next row: K.29 (31, 33, 35, 38) sts., turn and leave rem. sts. on a holder.
Cont. on these sts. only, dec. 1 st. at neck edge only on every row until 19 (21, 23, 25,28) sts. rem.
Work 5 (5, 5, 7, 9) rows straight.
Cast off.
With RS facing, slip first 16 (16, 16, 18, 18) sts. onto a holder.
Rejoin yarn and k. to end.
Complete 2nd side of neck to match first side, reversing all shaping.

SLEEVES

Using 3¼mm needles and grey, cast on 41 (45, 49, 53, 57) sts.
Work in k.1, p.1 rib as given for adult's sweater back for 6cm, ending with rib row 1.
Inc. row: Rib 3 (5, 7, 9, 11), m.1, * rib 6, m.1; rep from * to last 2 (4, 6, 8, 10) sts., rib to end: 48 (52, 56, 60, 64) sts.
Change to 4mm needles and cont. in st.st. inc. 1 st. at each end of 5th and every foll. 6th row until there are 72 (74, 80, 82, 88) sts.
Work straight until work measures 35 (37, 40, 43, 46) cm from beg.
Cast off.

NECKBAND

Join left shoulder seam.
Using 3¼mm needles and grey, with RS facing, pick up and k.11 (11, 11, 11, 12) sts. down right back neck, k. across 20 sts. from holder, pick up and k.12 (12, 12, 12, 13) sts. up left back neck, 17 (17, 17, 19, 21) sts. down left front neck, k. across 16 (16, 16, 18, 18) sts. from holder, pick up and k.17 (17, 17, 19, 21) sts. up right front neck: 93 (93, 93, 99, 105) sts.
P.1 row.
Rib row 1: K.1 med. gold, * p.1 grey, k.1 med. gold; rep. from * to end.
Rib row 2: P.1 med. gold, * k.1 grey, p.1 med. gold; rep. from * to end.
Rep. these 2 rib rows once more.
Rib row 5: K.1 med. gold, * p.1 dk. brown, k.1 med. gold; rep. from * to end.
Rib row 6: P.1 med. gold, * k.1 dk. brown, p.1 med. gold; rep. from * to end.
Using dk. brown, cast off in rib.

TO MAKE UP

Block and press pieces lightly under a damp cloth following ball band instructions. Join right shoulder and neckband seam. Joining cast-off edges of armholes to underarms of sleeves, sew in sleeves. Join side and sleeve seams.

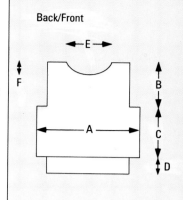

Back/Front

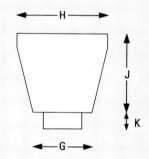

Sleeves

A 14¾ (15½; 16½; 17½; 18½) ins
37 (39; 41; 43.5; 46.5) cm
B 6½ (6¾; 7¼; 7½; 8) ins
16.5 (17; 18; 19; 20) cm
C 7½ (8; 9¼; 10½11½) ins
18.5 (20; 23; 26; 29) cm
D 2½ ins
6 cm
E 6½ (6½; 6½; 6½; 6¾) ins
16.5 (16.5; 16.5; 16.5; 17) cm
F 2 (2; 2; 2½; 2¾) ins
5 (5; 5; 6; 7) cm

G 8¾ (9½; 10¼; 11; 11½) ins
22 (24; 25.5; 27.5; 29) cm
H 13 (13½; 14½; 15½16) ins
32.5 (34; 36; 37; 40) cm
J 11¾ (12½; 13½; 14¾; 16) ins
29 (31; 34; 37; 40) cm
K 2½ ins
6 cm

The Swans familiar in ornamental parks are Mute Swans. These beautiful birds are residents in northern and central Europe and are still common, although they are subject to many hazards such as poisoning by leadweights used by fishermen, which they accidentally eat, or collision with overhead power cables. More rarely seen are the two smaller species, Bewick's Swan and the Whooping Swan. These breed in the high Arctic tundra and undergo long, hazar-dous migrations to winter in more southern regions, including the British Isles. Although a few are shot on these migrations, they have suffered mainly from the loss of their traditional wetland wintering sites through drainage of the land for conversion to agriculture. Fortunately several of the remaining wintering sites are now protected in nature reserves, such as that run by the Wildfowl Trust at Slimbridge in south-west England.

Whooper
SWANS
and Daffodils

▶ In strong sunlight, white swans take on a blue tinge when they stand in shadow. This classic cardigan in soft, grey cotton illustrates this well. Daffodils are added to the sleeves to reflect the yellow on the beaks of these Whooper Swans.

SIZES
To fit 75 (80, 85, 90, 95)cm – 30 (32, 34, 36, 38)in chest

MATERIALS
Pingouin Corrida 4 (DK cotton)
10 (10, 10, 11, 11) × 50g balls Tourterelle (shade 502)
1 × 50g ball each of Noir (528), Soleil (536), Blanc (501), Myosotis (508), Vert d'eau (543)
6 × 1.25cm (½in) crystal buttons
A pair each of 3¼mm (No. 10) and 4mm (No. 8) knitting needles
Stitch holder

TENSION
20 sts. and 26 rows to 10cm over st.st. worked on 4mm needles
Check your tension

NOTES
Instructions for larger sizes are given in brackets (   ).
When working motifs use separate, small balls of yarn.
When joining in a new colour, leave an end of about 5cm for darning in later, and when changing colour, twist yarns together at back of work to avoid making a hole.

If preferred, small areas, such as the grass, may be added later using Swiss darning; see 'Know-How' section.

BACK
Using 3¼mm needles and tourterelle, cast on 89 (95, 99, 105, 109) sts.
Rib row 1: K.1, * p.1, k.1; rep. from * to end.
Rib row 2: P.1 , * k.1, p.1; rep from * to end.
Rep. 2 rib rows for 2.5cm, inc. 1 st in last row: 90 (96, 100, 106, 110) sts.
Change to 4mm needles and work 36 (40, 40, 42, 46) rows st.st.
Then work rows 1–63 from Chart A.
Work 21 (23, 23, 27, 31) rows st.st.

Shape back neck
Next row: K.35, (38, 40, 43, 45), turn and leave rem. sts. on a stitch holder.
Work on these sts. only
Next row: Cast off 4 sts., p. to end.
K.1 row.
Next row: Cast off 4 (4, 5, 5, 6) sts., p. to end.
Cast off rem. 27 (30, 31, 34, 35) sts.
Return to rem. sts.

'Swans and Daffodils'
modelled by actress
Elizabeth Hurley, who
recently starred in the BBC
series Cristobel. Elizabeth
lives in South Kensington
and is soon to star in the
American mini-series Act
of Will.

SWANS AND DAFFODILS

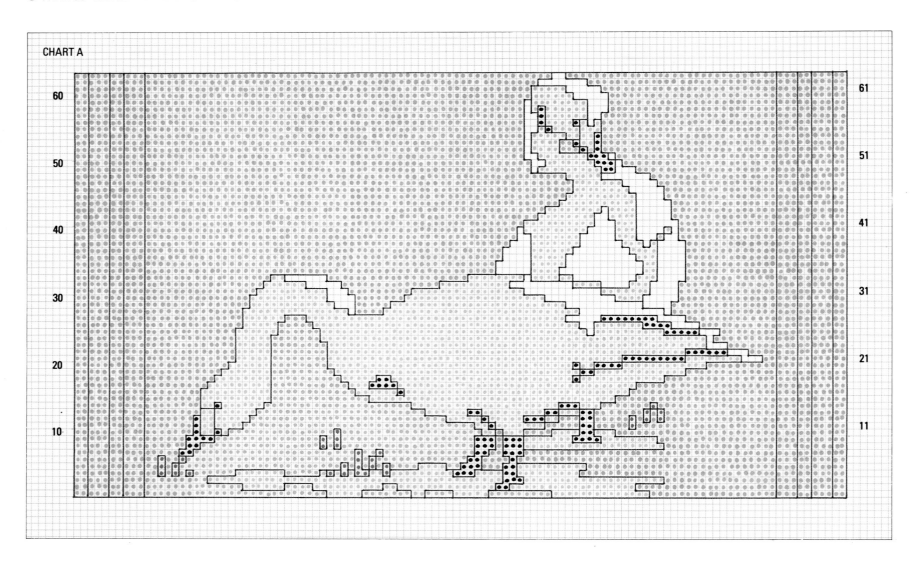

CHART A

- Tourterelle (502)
- Noir (528)
- Soleil (536)
- Blanc (501)
- Myosotis (508)
- Vert D'eau (543)

With RS facing, slip first 20 sts. onto a stitch holder.

Rejoin yarn to first st. and k. to end.

Complete to match first side of back neck, reversing all shaping.

LEFT FRONT

** Using 3¼mm needles and tourterelle, cast on 45 (47, 49, 53, 55) sts.

Work 2.5cm in rib as given for back.

For 2nd and 3rd sizes only, inc. 1 st. in last row: 45 (48, 50, 53, 55) sts. **

Change to 4mm needles and work 8 (12, 12, 14, 18) rows st.st.

Then work rows 1–92 from Chart B.

Work 8 (10, 10, 14, 18) rows st.st.

Shape front neck

Next row: K.35, (38, 40, 43, 45) sts., turn and leave rem. sts. on a stitch holder.

*** Work on these sts. only, dec 1 st. at neck edge only until 27 (30, 31, 34, 35) sts. rem.

Work 7 (7, 6, 6, 5) rows straight.

Cast off ***.

RIGHT FRONT

Work as given for left front from ** to **.

Change to 4mm needles and work 46 (50, 50, 52, 56) rows st.st.

Work rows 1–35 from Chart C.

Work 28 (30, 30, 34, 38) rows straight, ending with a k. row.

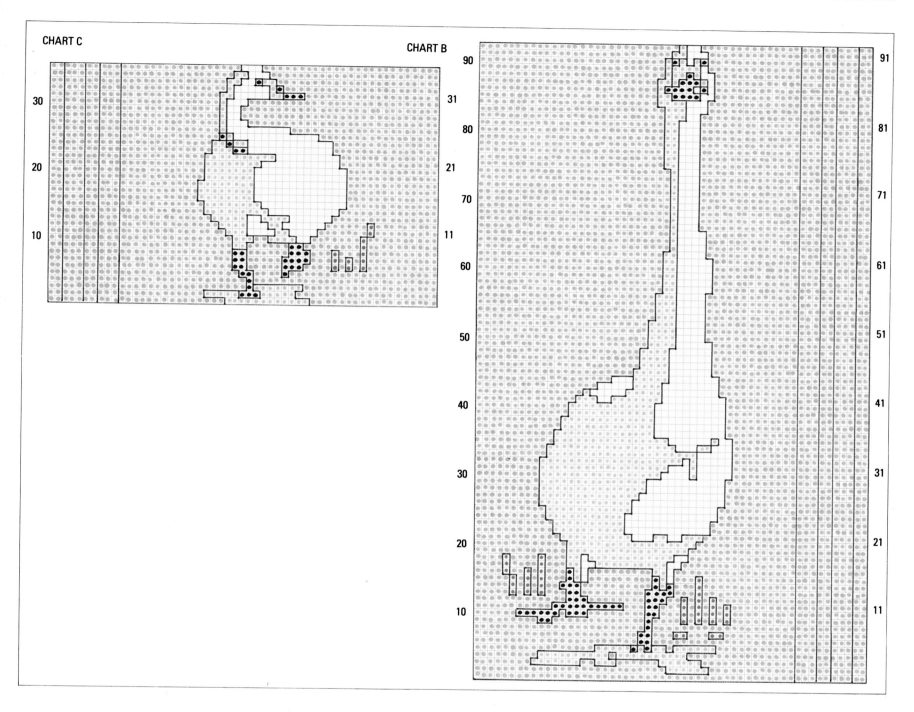

CHART C   **CHART B**

Shape front neck

Next row: P.35, (38, 40, 43, 45) sts., turn and leave rem. sts. on a stitch holder. Now cont. as given for left front from *** to ***.

SLEEVES

Using 3¼mm needles and tourterelle, cast on 45 (47, 47, 49, 49) sts.

Work 2 cm in rib as given for back, inc. 1 st. at end of last row: 46 (48, 48, 50, 50) sts.

Change to 4mm needles and work from row 1 of Chart D, at the same time, inc. 1 st. each end of 5th and every foll. 4th row until there are 86 (90, 90, 92, 92) sts.

Work straight until row 88 of chart has been completed.

For 1st, 2nd and 3rd sizes only, work 16 (20, 22) rows straight. Cast off.

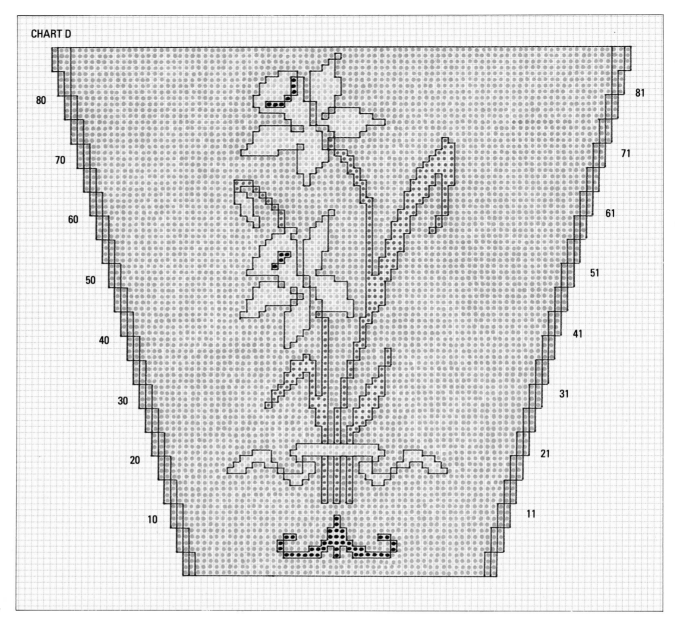

CHART D

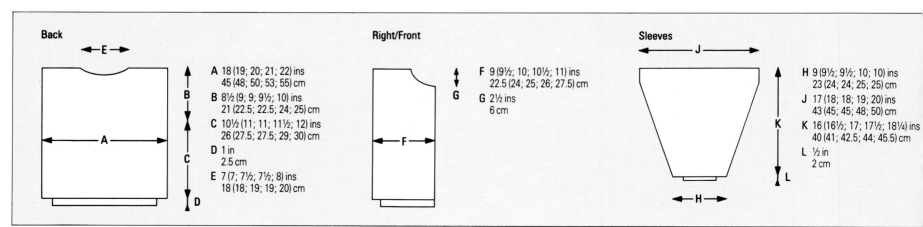

Back

A 18 (19; 20; 21; 22) ins
45 (48; 50; 53; 55) cm

B 8½ (9; 9; 9½; 10) ins
21 (22.5; 22.5; 24; 25) cm

C 10½ (11; 11; 11½; 12) ins
26 (27.5; 27.5; 29; 30) cm

D 1 in
2.5 cm

E 7 (7; 7½; 7½; 8) ins
18 (18; 19; 19; 20) cm

Right/Front

F 9 (9½; 10; 10½; 11) ins
22.5 (24; 25; 26; 27.5) cm

G 2½ ins
6 cm

Sleeves

H 9 (9½; 9½; 10; 10) ins
23 (24; 24; 25; 25) cm

J 17 (18; 18; 19; 20) ins
43 (45; 45; 48; 50) cm

K 16 (16½; 17; 17½; 18¼) ins
40 (41; 42.5; 44; 45.5) cm

L ½ in
2 cm

For 4th and 5th sizes only, cont. inc. as before until there are 96 (100) sts.

Work 21 (17) rows straight.

Cast off.

NECK BAND

Join shoulder seams.

Using 3¼mm needles and tourterelle, with RS facing, starting at right front, k.10 sts. from holder, pick up and k.17 sts. up right front neck, 12 (12, 13, 13, 13) sts. down right back neck, k.20 sts. from holder, pick up and k.13 (13, 14, 14, 14) sts. up left back neck, 17 sts. down left front neck, k.10 sts. from holder: 99 (99, 101, 101, 101) sts.

P.1 row.

Work 4 rows rib as given for back.

Cast off in rib.

BUTTONBAND

Using 3¼mm needles and tourterelle, with RS facing, pick up and k.91 (97, 97, 101, 107) sts. down left front edge.

Starting rib row 2, work 5 rows rib as given for back.

Cast off in rib.

BUTTONHOLE BAND

Using 3¼mm needles and tourterelle, with RS facing, pick up and k.91 (97, 97, 101, 107) sts. up right front edge.

Starting rib row 2, rib 1 row as given for back.

Next row: Rib 2 (3, 3, 2, 2), cast off 2 sts., * rib 15 (16, 16, 17, 18), cast off 2 sts.; rep. from * to last 2 (2, 2, 2, 3) sts., rib to end.

Next row: Rib 2 (2, 2, 2, 3), cast on 2 sts. * rib 15 (16, 16, 17, 18), cast on 2 sts.; rep. from * to last 2 (3, 3, 2, 2) sts., rib to end.

Work 2 rows rib.

Cast off in rib.

TO MAKE UP

Block and press pieces lightly under a damp cloth foll. ball band instructions. Sew in sleeves. Join side and sleeve seams. Sew on buttons to correspond with buttonholes.

Whales are found in all the major oceans of the world and include the largest animal that has ever lived, the one-hundred-foot long Blue Whale. Mankind has long regarded Whales as valuable sources of oil and meat, and for many years they have been intensively harvested. As a result populations which once numbered in their hundreds of thousands, have been reduced to a tiny fraction of this.

Increasing concern about the future of Whales reached the point that in 1986 a temporary ban on all large-scale commercial whaling was declared. The rarest and most endangered Whale, the Bowhead, found in the cold northern waters of the Atlantic and Pacific, is still threatened by small-scale hunting carried out by Eskimos in the Bering Straits region of Alaska.

ORCAS
Breaching Whales

▶ These chunky oversized sweaters have a definite 'marine' feel to them. Bands of jacquard and the phrases 'Extinction Is Forever' and 'Save The Whale' feature on the back and sleeves. The main motif depicts a 'Breaching Whale'. A simple cable design completes the effect.

SIZES
Men's sweater (Blue colourway): one size only to fit 80 to 105cm – 32 to 42in chest.
Ladies' sweater (Grey colourway): one size only to fit 80 to 105cm – 32 to 42in chest.

MATERIALS
Men's sweater
Pingouin Chunky
9 × 50g balls Marine (shade 15)
4 × 50g balls each of Ecru (shade 10) and Noir (shade 16)
Pingouin Mohican, flecked chunky
7 × 50g balls Souris (shade 11)
Pingouin Star + (used double)
2 × 50g balls Violet (shade 26)
Ladies' sweater
Pingouin Mohican, flecked chunky
9 × 50g balls Souris (shade 11)
Pingouin Chunky
6 × 50g balls Ecru (shade 10)
3 × 50g balls each of Noir (shade 16) and Marine (shade 15)

Pingouin Star + (used double)
3 × 50g balls Violet (shade 26)
A pair each of 5mm (No. 6) and 6mm (No. 4) knitting needles
Stitch holder

TENSION
13 sts. and 16 rows to 10cm over jacquard patt. worked on 6mm needles
Check your tension

NOTES
When working motif, use separate small balls of yarn. When joining in a new colour, leave an end of about 5cm for darning in later and when changing colour, twist yarns together at back of work to avoid making a hole.

ABBREVIATIONS
CR2R – cross 2 sts. to the right: k. into front of 2nd st., then k. first st.

'Orcas' modelled by actor Michael Palin. Ex-Monty Python, Michael Palin has starred in many international motion pictures, such as The Missionary *and* A Fish Called Wanda.

ORCAS

Colourway 1

● Marine (15)
● Souris (11)
● Noir (16)
● Violet (26)
□ Ecru (10)

Colourway 2

● Souris (11)
● Ecru (10)
● Violet (26)
● Noir (16)
□ Marine (15)

Men's sweater

BACK

** With 5mm needles and marine, cast on 68 sts.
Work cabled rib as follows:
Rib row 1: K.1 , p.2, * k.2, p.2; rep. from * to last st., k.1.
Rib row 2: P.1, k.2, * p.2, k.2; rep. from * to last st., p.1.
Rib row 3: K.1, p.2, * CR2R, p.2; rep. from * to last st., k.1.
Rib row 4: As row 2.
Rep. these 4 rows twice more, then work row 1.
Inc. row: Rib 4, m.1, * rib 5, m.1; rep. from * to last 4 sts, rib to end: 81 sts.

Change to 6mm needles and work rows 5–20 from Chart B **.
Work rows 1–10 of Chart D, placing chart after first 10 sts of souris. Then work rows 1–20 from Chart B, then work Chart E placing chart after first 33 sts. of souris.
Rep Chart B, then rows 1–10 from Chart F.
Then work rows 1–5 from Chart B.
Next row: Using marine, p.2 tog., p. to end: 80 sts.
*** Using 6mm needles and marine, work 12 rows of cabled rib as welt.
Next row: Cast off 26 sts., k.28, cast off 26 sts.
Leave rem 28 sts. on a stitch holder.

CHART B

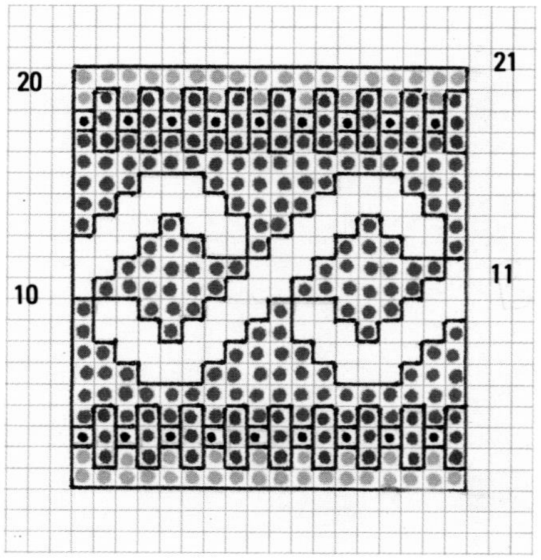

CHART G

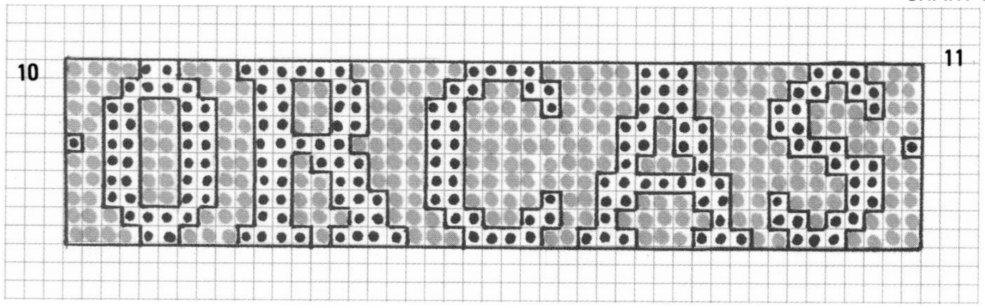

CHART F

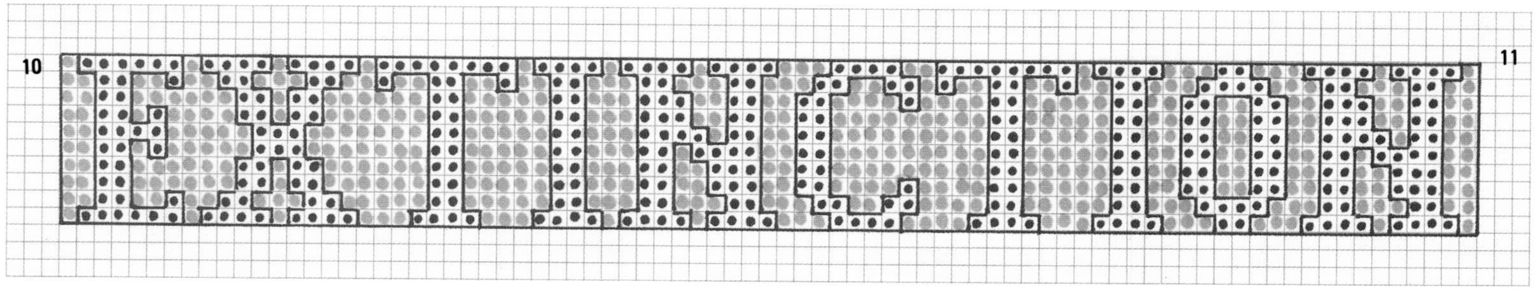

CHART E

CHART D

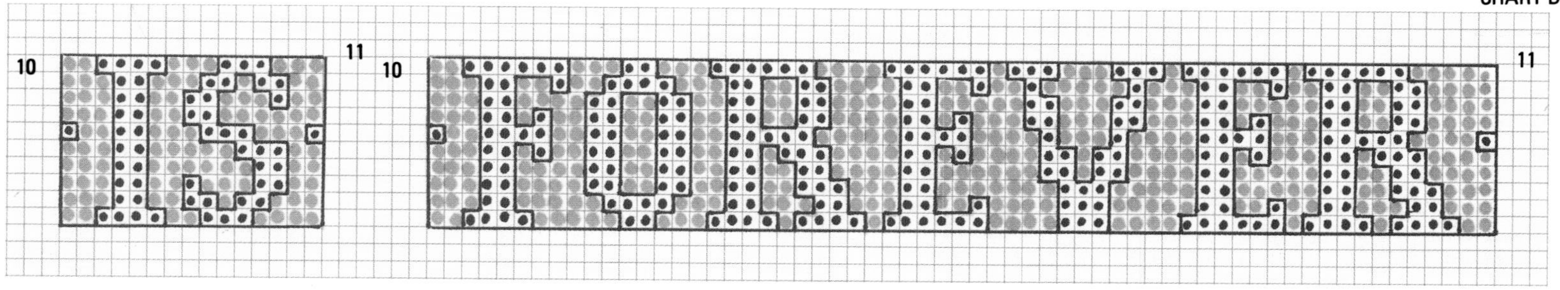

FRONT

Work as given for back from ** to **.

Then work rows 1–53 from Chart A.

Using marine, work 3 rows st.st., then work rows 17–20 from Chart B.

Place Chart G after first 18 sts. of souris.

Work rows 1–5 from Chart B.

Next row: With marine, p.2 tog., p. to end: 80 sts.

Shape front neck

*** Using 6mm needles, work in cable rib as given for back welt:

Next row: Rib 33, turn and leave remaining sts. on a stitch holder.

Work on these sts. only.

Keeping cable patt. correct, dec. 1 st. at neck edge only on every row until 26 sts. remain.

Work 4 rows without shaping. Cast off in rib.

Return to remaining sts.

With RS facing, slip first 14 sts. onto a stitch holder.

Rejoin yarn and keeping patt. correct, work to end.

Now complete to match first side of neck, reversing all shaping.

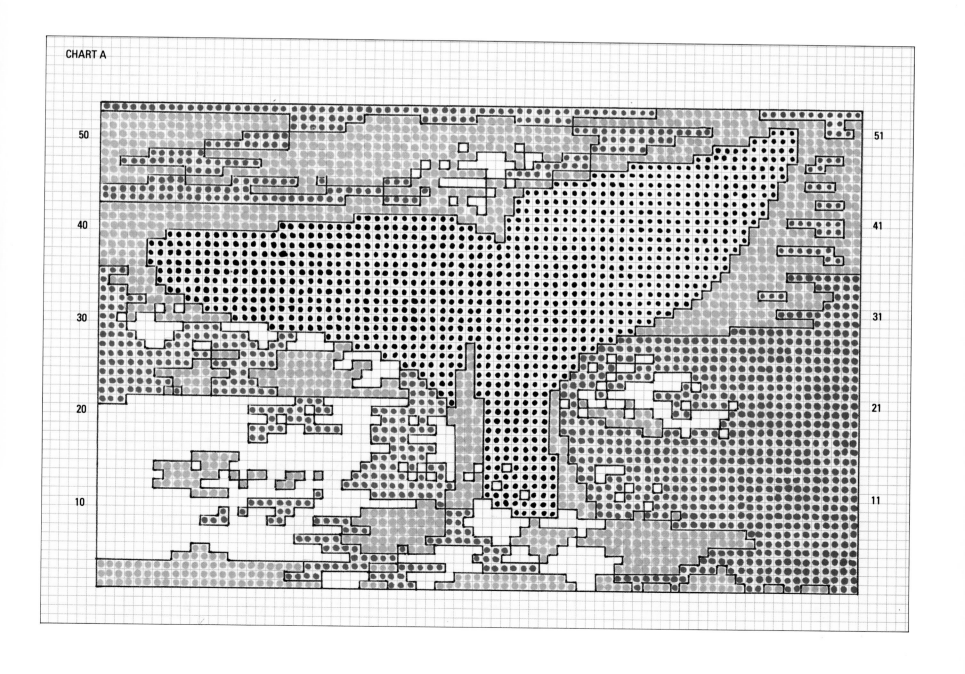

CHART A

SLEEVES

Using 5mm needles and marine, cast on 32 sts.

Rep. the 4 cable rib rows as given for back twice, then work row 1.

Inc. row: Rib 1, * m.1, rib 3; rep. from * to last st., rib 1: 43 sts.

Change to 6mm needles and work in patt from Chart H, working sleeve shaping as indicated until row 74 has been worked: 73 sts.

Cast off.

COLLAR

Join left shoulder seam.

With RS facing, using 5mm needles and marine, k. across 28 sts. of back neck; pick up and k.13 sts. down left front; k. across 14 sts. of front neck; pick up and k.13 sts. up right front: 68 sts.

Rib row 1: K.1, p.2. * k.2, * p.2; rep. from * to last st., k.1

Rib row 2: P.1, CR2R, * p.2, CR2R; rep. from * to last st., p.1.

Rib row 3: As row 1.

Rib row 4: P.1, k.2, * p.2, k.2; rep. from * to last st., p.1.

Rep 4 cable rib rows twice more.

Cast off in rib.

TO MAKE UP

Block and press pieces lightly under a damp cloth following ball band instructions. Join right shoulder and collar seams. Sew in sleeves. Then join side and sleeve seams.

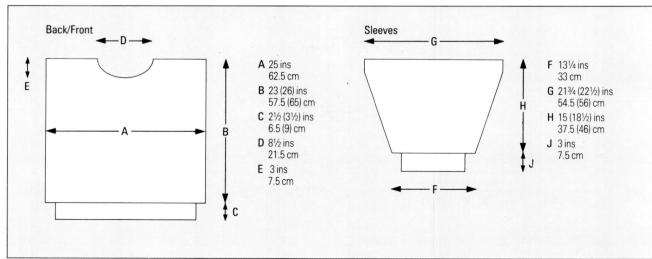

Back/Front

A 25 ins
62.5 cm

B 23 (26) ins
57.5 (65) cm

C 2½ (3½) ins
6.5 (9) cm

D 8½ ins
21.5 cm

E 3 ins
7.5 cm

Sleeves

F 13¼ ins
33 cm

G 21¾ (22½) ins
54.5 (56) cm

H 15 (18½) ins
37.5 (46) cm

J 3 ins
7.5 cm

CHART H

'Orcas' modelled by Susan George, who has starred in over thirty motion pictures, most notably Peckinpah's Straw Dogs. She is currently producing films with her company, Amy International Productions.

Ladies' sweater

Note: Follow 2nd Colourway to work Charts B, D, E, F, G and H.

BACK

** Using 5mm needles and souris, cast on 68 sts.
Rep. the 4 rib rows as given for men's back, twice.
Then work rib row 1. Work inc. row as before: 81 sts.
Change to 6mm needles.
Work rows 17–20 from Chart B.**
Then position Charts D and E side by side as follows:
Row 1: K.1 ecru, k. row 1 from Chart D, k.3 ecru, k. row 1 from Chart E, k.1 ecru.
When these 10 rows have been completed, * work from Chart B, then Chart C; rep from * once more.
Then work rows 1–5 from Chart B.
Next row: Using souris, p.2 tog., p. to end: 80 sts.
Complete in souris as for men's back from *** to end.

FRONT

Work as given for ladies' back from ** to **.
Work Chart F, then work rows 1–4 from Chart B.

Work rows 1–53 from Chart A, then 2 rows st.st. using marine.
Next row: P.1 marine * p.1 noir, p.1 marine; rep. from * to end.
Work rows 3–5 from Chart B.
Using souris, work 1 row st.st., dec. 1 st. at beg. of row: 80 sts.
Now complete as given for men's front from *** to end, using souris.

SLEEVES

Using 5mm needles and souris, cast on 32 sts.
Work cuffs and rows 1–34 from Chart H as given for men's sleeves: 43sts.
Now set chart C as follows:
Row 1: K.5 ecru * k.1 violet, k.5 ecru; rep. from * to end.
Continue shaping sleeves as before and complete Chart C.
Then work rows 45–60 from Chart H: 71 sts.
Cast off.

COLLAR

Using souris, work collar as given for men's collar.

TO MAKE UP

As given for men's sweater.

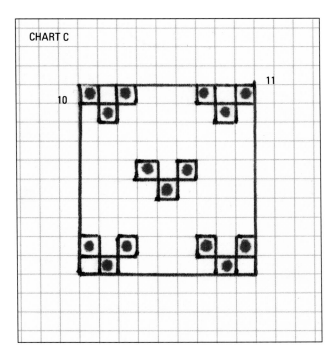

Soaring over mountains and forests, the Golden Eagle is without doubt one of the most majestic of all birds. It is also one of the most widespread, being found through much of the northern hemisphere, particularly in temperate regions of North America, Europe and Asia. Unfortunately, wherever Golden Eagles are found they come into conflict with farmers who accuse them of preying on new-born lambs. As a consequence they have been poisoned and trapped, and even shot from aeroplanes, in large numbers. They have also, like all birds of prey, suffered from the excessive use of pesticides which build up in the food they eat and can cause them to lay infertile or thin-shelled and easily broken eggs. Improved environmental controls have decreased this problem to some extent in recent years. This, and the legal protection now given to Golden Eagles in many countries has allowed some populations to start recovering slowly.

Golden EAGLE

▶ This tunic-style sweater is emblazoned with stitchery, beading and embroidery. The design focuses on the intense and sharp-sighted eyes of this magnificent bird of prey – its right wing unfolding, it is aware of danger. The Celtic patterning complements the Eagle's colouring.

SIZES
To fit 80 (85, 90, 95)cm – 32 (34, 36, 38)in chest.

MATERIALS
Emu Superwash DK 100% wool
9 (9, 10, 10) × 50g balls Dk Grey (shade 3071)
2 × 50g balls each of Black (shade 3070), Dk Gold (3019)
1 × 50g ball each of Green (shade 3075), Purple (3052), Lt Grey (3080), Brown (3009), White (3078), Lt Gold (3006) and Dk Brown (3011)
A pair each of 3¼mm (No. 10) and 4mm (No. 8) knitting needles
Small beads
Stitch holder

TENSION
23 sts. and 27 rows to 10cm over st.st. patt. worked on 4mm needles
Check your tension

ABBREVIATIONS
CR2R: cross 2 sts. to the right – k. into front of 2nd st., then k. 1st st.
CR2L: cross 2 sts. to the left – k. into back of 2nd st., then k. first st.
Sl.1 – slip 1 st. purlwise.

FEATHER STITCH (over 18 sts.)
Row 1: * K.8, p. 1; rep. from * to end.
Row 2: * K.1, p.8; rep. from * to end.
Row 3: * K.8, p.3, CR2R, CR2L, p.3; rep. from * to end.
Row 4: * K.3, sl.1, p.2, sl.1, k.3, p.8; rep. from * to end.
Row 5: * K.8, p.2, CR2R, k.2, CR2L, p.2; rep. from * to end.
Row 6: * K.2, sl.1, p.4, sl.1, k.2, p.8; rep. from * to end.
Row 7: * K.8, p.1, CR2R, k.4, CR2L, p.1; rep. from * to end.
Row 8: * K.1, sl.1, p.6, sl.1, k.1, p.8; rep. from * to end.
Row 9: As row 1.
Row 10: As row 2.
Row 11: * P.2, CR2R, CR2L, p.3, k.8, p.1; rep. from * to end.
Row 12: K.1, p.8, k.3, sl.1, p.2, sl.1, k.2; rep. from * to end.
Row 13: * P.1, CR2R, k.2, CR2L, p.2, k.8, p.1; rep. from * to end.
Row 14: * K.1, p.8, k.2, sl.1, p.4, sl.1, k.1; rep. from *to end.
Row 15: * CR2R, k.4, CR2L, p.1, k.8, p.1; rep. from * to end.
Row 16: * K.1, p.8, k.1, sl.1, p.6, sl.1; rep. from * to end.
These 16 rows form pattern.

'Golden Eagle' modelled by multi-lingual actress Rula Lenska, who has appeared in countless TV and theatre productions. Rula is passionate about conservation and dedicates a lot of her spare time to the WWF. She is also the narrator on Anglia TVs production Survival.

NOTES

Instructions for the larger sizes are given in brackets ( ).
When working motif, use separate, small balls of yarn.
When joining in a new colour, leave an end of about 5cm
for darning in later, and when changing colour, twist yarns
together at back of work to avoid making a hole.

BACK

** Using 3¼mm needles and black, cast on 103 (109, 115,
121) sts.

Rib row 1: K.1 dk. grey, * p.1 black, k.1 dk. grey; rep. from *
to end.

Rib row 2: P.1 dk. grey, * k.1 black, p.1 dk. grey; rep. from *
to end.

Rep. these 2 rows once more, inc. 1 st. at end of last row:
104 (110, 116, 122) sts.

Change to 4mm needles and work rows 1–58 from
Chart A. **

Row 59: Work row 1 of feather st., placing patt. as folls: K.2
(5, 8, 2), p.1, * k.8, p.1; rep. from * to last 2 (5, 8, 2) sts., k. to
end.

Row 60: Keeping patt. correct, work from row 2 of feather
patt.

Cont. in feather st. until 4 complete reps. have been
worked, then work rows 1–8 once more.

Shape armholes

Cast off 4 sts. at beg. of next 2 rows. Cont. working feather
st. patt. on rem. 96 (102, 108, 114) sts. until 6 complete
patt. reps. have been worked, then work rows 1 and 2 once
more.

Work rows 1–46 (46, 48, 52) from Chart C.

Shape back neck

Next row: K.36 (38, 40, 42), turn and leave rem. sts. on a
stitch holder.

Work on these sts. only.

Next row: Cast off 5 sts., p. to end.

K.1 row.

Cast off 6 sts., p. to end.

Cast off.

Return to rem. sts.

With RS facing, slip first 24 (26, 28, 30) sts. onto a holder.
Rejoin yarn to first st. and k. to end.

Complete 2nd side of back neck to match first side,
reversing all shaping.

FRONT

Work as given for back from ** to **
Work 2 rows in dk. grey.

Work rows 1–96 from Chart B, shaping armholes at beg. of
rows 71 and 72: 96 (102, 108, 114) sts.

Now work rows 1–28 (28, 30, 34) from Chart C.

Shape front neck

Next row: Working in patt., k.38 (41, 44, 47), turn and
leave rem.sts. on a spare needle.

Work on these sts. only.

Dec. 1 st. at neck edge only until 25 (27, 29, 31) sts. rem.

Work 8 (7, 6, 5) rows straight.

Cast off.

Return to rem. sts.

With RS facing, slip first 20 sts. onto holder.

Rejoin yarn to first st., k. to end.

Complete 2nd side of front neck to match first side,
reversing all shaping.

◉	(3071)
●	(3070)
◉	(3019)
◉	(3011)
☐	(3078)
◉	(3080)
◉	(3052)
◉	(3075)
◉	(3009)
◉	(3006)
☒	Cross stitch using black (3070)

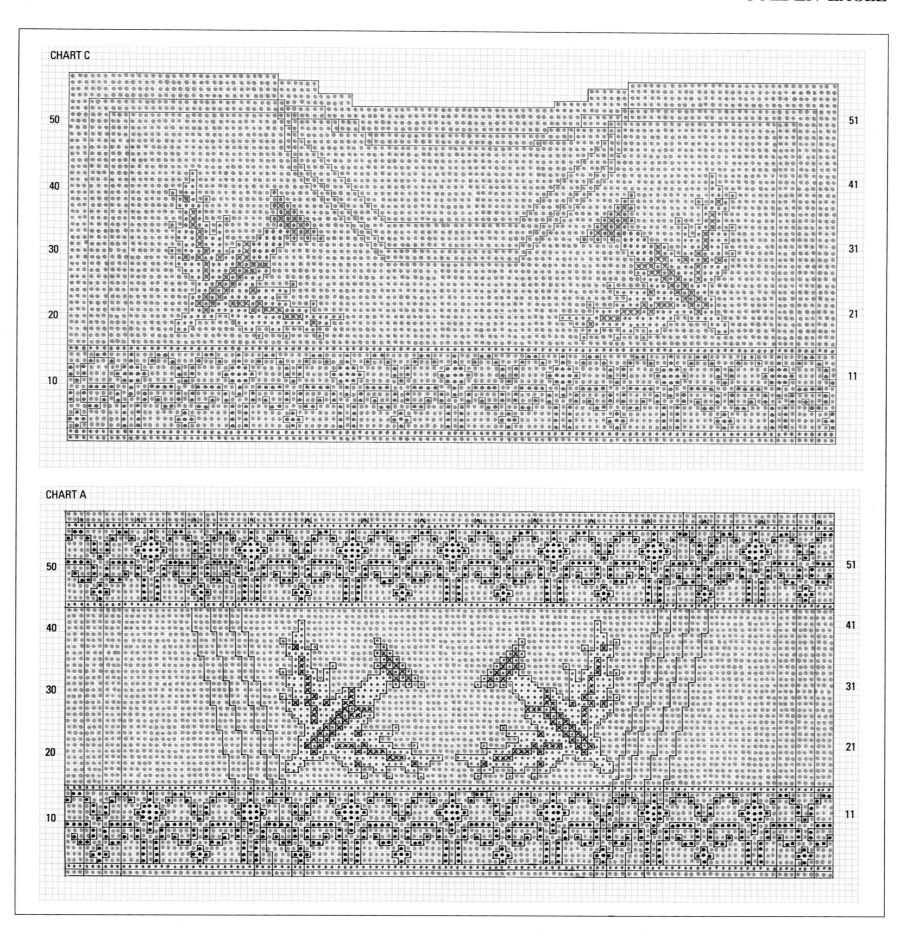

GOLDEN EAGLE

CHART B

SLEEVES

Using 3¼mm needles and black, cast on 45 (49, 55, 61) sts.

Rep. 2 rib rows as given for back twice, inc. 1 st. at end of last row: 46 (50, 56, 62) sts.

Change to 4mm needles and work from row 1 of Chart A, shaping sleeve by inc. 1 st. each end of 5th and every foll. 4th row until there are 74 (78, 84, 90) sts.

Change to dk. grey.

Row 59: Work row 1 of feather st. placing patt. as folls.: k.5 (7, 1, 4), p.1, * k.8, p.1; rep. from * to last 5 (7, 1, 4) sts., k. to end.

Row 60: Keeping patt. correct, work row 2 of feather st. patt.

Cont. from row 3 of feather st. patt. and at same time, inc. 1 st. each end of next and every foll. 4th row until there are

110 (110, 116, 122) sts., taking all inc. sts. into feather st. patt.

Work 11 (19, 19, 19) rows straight.

Cast off.

COLLAR

Join left shoulder seam.

Using 3¼mm needles and dk. grey, pick up and k.9 sts. down right back neck, k. across 24 (26, 28, 30) sts. from holder, pick up and k.10 sts. up left back neck, pick up and k.21 sts. down left front neck, k. across 20 sts. from holder, pick up and k.21 sts. up right front neck: 105 (107, 109, 111) sts.

Rib row 1: Using dk. grey, p.1, * k.1, p.1; rep. from * to end.

Rib row 2: K.1 black, * p.1 dk. grey, k.1 black; rep. from * to end.

Rib row 3: P.1 black, * k.1 dk.grey, p.1 black; rep. from * to end.

Rib row 4: K.1 black, * p.1 purple, k.1 black; rep. from * to end.

Rib row 5: P.1 black, * k.1 purple, p.1 black; rep. from * to end.

Rep rows 4 and 5, 4 more times.

Using black, cast off.

TO MAKE UP

Block and press pieces lightly under a damp cloth foll. ball band instructions. Join right shoulder and collar seam. Work backstitch embroidery and French knots as indicated on Chart B. Using black, Swiss darn thistles as indicated on Charts A and C. Joining cast-off edge of armholes to underarms of sleeves, sew in sleeves, then join side and sleeve seams. Sew on pairs of beads at points of feather stitch on back and sleeves.

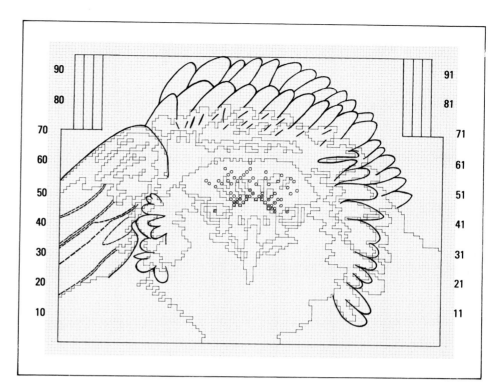

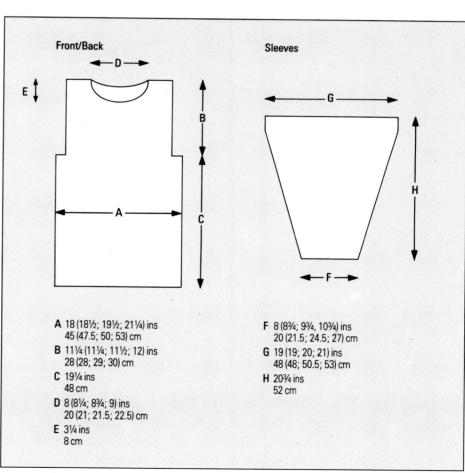

Backstitch embroidery using Black (3070)	French Knot using Black (3070)
Backstitch embroidery using White (3078)	French Knot using Lt. Grey (3080)
Backstitch embroidery using Lt. Gold (3006)	

Front/Back

Sleeves

A 18 (18½; 19½; 21¼) ins
45 (47.5; 50; 53) cm

B 11¼ (11¼; 11½; 12) ins
28 (28; 29; 30) cm

C 19¼ ins
48 cm

D 8 (8¼; 8¾; 9) ins
20 (21; 21.5; 22.5) cm

E 3¼ ins
8 cm

F 8 (8¾; 9¾, 10¾) ins
20 (21.5; 24.5; 27) cm

G 19 (19; 20; 21) ins
48 (48; 50.5; 53) cm

H 20¾ ins
52 cm

Running for 1,200 miles off the coast of Queensland in eastern Australia, the Great Barrier Reef is the world's largest coral reef and one of the most colourful places on earth. Like all such reefs it is made up of the stony skeletons of millions of tiny coral polyps. The coral colonies grow in an extraordinary variety of shapes to produce fantastic underwater landscapes which support myriad other forms of life, including fish, lobsters, starfish and sea-shells of all description. Coral reefs are only found in shallow tropical sea water and are threatened everywhere by mining for sand and coral rock for building, pollution, and destructive fishing methods including dynamiting and poisoning. Fortunately most of the Great Barrier Reef is included in a national park where man's activities are carefully controlled and visitors can enjoy the reef's unparalleled beauties without destroying them.

Great
BARRIER REEF

▶ The exotic shape of this little dress is the perfect choice for this tropical theme. The soft cotton yarn and stitchery provide the wealth of colour and texture needed to portray the riches of the coral reef.

SIZES
To fit 80 (85, 90)cm – 32 (34, 36)in chest

MATERIALS
Pingouin Corrida 4 (DK cotton)
8 (8, 9) × 50g balls Noir (shade 528).
1 × 50g ball each of Tourterelle (502), Soleil (536), Corail (542), Lagon (517), Feu (514), Myosotis (508), Vert d'eau (543)
A pair each of 3¼mm (No. 10) and 4mm (No. 8) knitting needles
One 3¼mm (No. 10) circular knitting needle
Stitch holder

TENSION
20 sts. and 26 rows to 10cm over patt. worked on 4mm needles
Check your tension

NOTES
Instructions for larger sizes are given in brackets ( ).
When working motifs use separate, small balls of yarn.
When joining in a new colour, leave an end of about 5cm for darning in later. When changing colour, twist yarns together at back of work to avoid making a hole.

ABBREVIATIONS
See key on diagram
Nobble – (K.1, k.1 tbl, k.1) all in same stitch, turn, p.3, turn, k.3 tog.
CR2R – K. into front of 2nd st., then k. first st.
CR2L – K. into back of 2nd st., then k. first st.

BACK
** Using 3¼mm needles and noir, cast on 83 (89, 95) sts.
Rib row 1: K.1, * p.1, k.1; rep from * to end.
Rib row 2: P.1, * k.1, p.1; rep. from * to end.
Rep. 2 rib rows twice more, then row 1 once more.
Change to 4mm needles.
Dec. row: P.5 (3, 7), p.2 tog., * p.5 (6, 6), p.2 tog.; rep from * to last 6 (4, 6) sts., p. to end: 72 (78, 84) sts.
Work 10 rows st.st.
Work from row 1 of Chart A, shaping sides as indicated on chart, ** until row 160 has been completed: 70 (74, 78) sts.

Shape back neck

Next row: Work 25 (27, 29) sts. in patt., turn and leave rem. sts. on a holder.

Work on these sts. only.

Next row: Cast off 3 sts., patt. to end. Keeping patt. correct, cast off 2 sts. at beg. of foll. 4 alt. rows. Then dec. 1 st. at beg. of foll. 6 (7, 8) alt. rows: 8 (9, 10) sts.

Work 8 rows straight.

*** *Next row:* Cast off 4 (5, 5) sts., k. to end.

P.1 row.

Cast off rem. 4 (4, 5) sts.

With RS facing, slip first 20 sts. onto a holder ***.

Rejoin yarn to first st. and k. to end.

Complete 2nd side of back neck to match first side, reversing all shaping.

FRONT

Work as given for back from ** to **, then cont. from chart until row 148 has been completed: 72 (76, 80) sts.

Shape front neck

Next row: K.2, k.2 tog., k.22 (24, 26) sts., turn and leave rem sts. on a stitch holder.

Work on these sts. only.

Next row: Cast off 4 sts., p. to end.

Cast off 3 sts. at beg. of next alt. row.

Then, keeping patt. correct, cast off 2 sts. at beg. of foll. 3 alt. rows, then dec. 1 st. at beg. of foll. 4 (5, 6) alt. rows: 8 (9, 10) sts.

Work 24 rows straight, then work as given for back from *** to ***

Rejoin yarn to first st. and k. to last 4 sts., k.2 tog. tbl, k.2.

Complete 2nd side of front neck to match first side, reversing all shaping.

RIGHT SLEEVE

** Using 3¼mm needles and noir, cast on 57 (61, 65) sts.

Work 5 rows rib as given for back.

Change to 4mm needles.

Dec. row: P.6 (6, 4), p.2 tog., * p.5 (6, 7), p.2 tog.; rep. from * to last 7 (5, 5) sts., p. to end **: 50 (54, 58) sts.

*'Great Barrier Reef'
modelled by Marie Helvin.*

GREAT BARRIER REEF

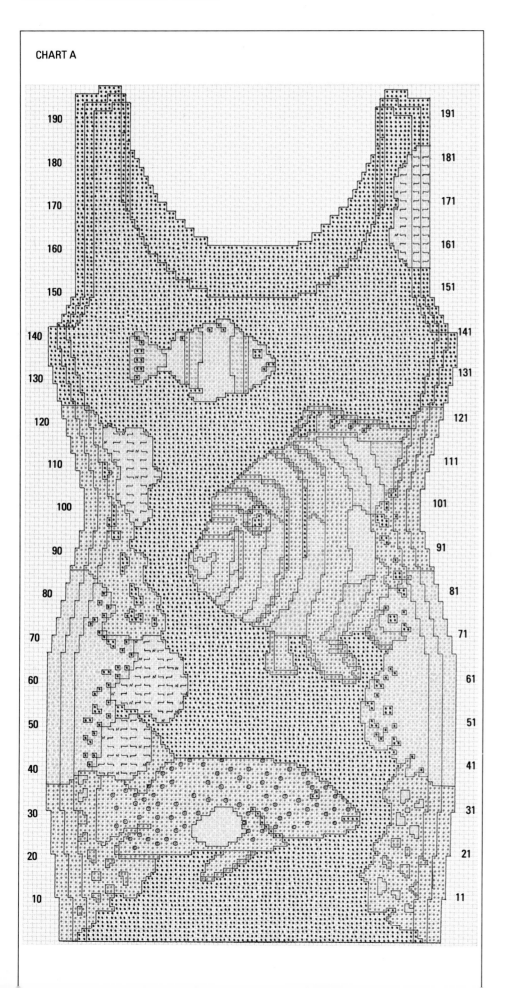

CHART A

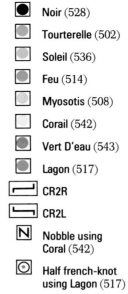

190
180
170
160
150
140
130
120
110
100
90
80
70
60
50
40
30
20
10

191
181
171
161
151
141
131
121
111
101
91
81
71
61
51
41
31
21
11

● Noir (528)

● Tourterelle (502)

● Soleil (536)

● Feu (514)

● Myosotis (508)

□ Corail (542)

● Vert D'eau (543)

● Lagon (517)

⌐ CR2R

⌐ CR2L

Ⓝ Nobble using
Coral (542)

⊙ Half french-knot
using Lagon (517)

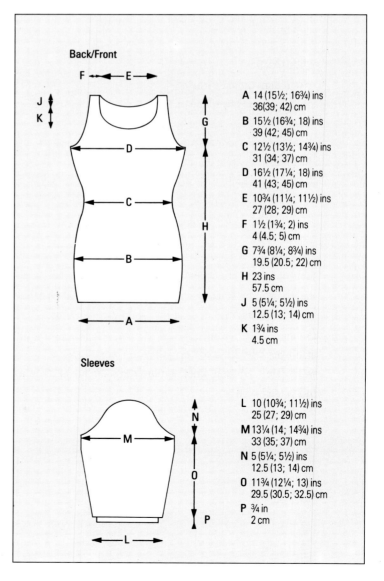

Back/Front

F ↔ E

J ↕
K ↕

A 14 (15½; 16¾) ins
36 (39; 42) cm

B 15½ (16¾; 18) ins
39 (42; 45) cm

C 12½ (13½; 14¾) ins
31 (34; 37) cm

D 16½ (17¼; 18) ins
41 (43; 45) cm

E 10¾ (11¼; 11½) ins
27 (28; 29) cm

F 1½ (1¾; 2) ins
4 (4.5; 5) cm

G 7¾ (8¼; 8¾) ins
19.5 (20.5; 22) cm

H 23 ins
57.5 cm

J 5 (5¼; 5½) ins
12.5 (13; 14) cm

K 1¾ ins
4.5 cm

Sleeves

L 10 (10¾; 11½) ins
25 (27; 29) cm

M 13¼ (14; 14¾) ins
33 (35; 37) cm

N 5 (5¼; 5½) ins
12.5 (13; 14) cm

O 11¾ (12¼; 13) ins
29.5 (30.5; 32.5) cm

P ¾ in
2 cm

Cont. in st.st. inc. 1 st. at each end of 5th and every foll. 8th row until there are 62 (66, 72) sts.

Work 1 (5, 1) rows. Then work rows 55–84 from Chart B.

Shape raglan

*** Cast off 2 sts. at beg. of next 4 rows. Then keeping patt. correct, dec 1 st. at beg. of every row until 40 (44, 48) sts. rem.

Then cast off 2 sts. at beg. of next 6 (8, 10) rows and 3 sts. at beg. of foll. 4 rows.

Cast off rem. 16 sts. ***

LEFT SLEEVE

Work as given for right sleeve from ** to **.

Work from row 9 (5, 1) to row 51 of Chart B, at the same time, shape sleeve by inc. 1 st. each end of 5th and every foll. 8th row until there are 66 (70, 74) sts.

Work 15 (19, 23) rows straight.

Cont. as given for right sleeve from *** to ***.

NECKBAND

Join left shoulder seam.

Using 3¼mm circular knitting needle and noir, with RS facing, pick up and k.39 (40, 41) sts. down right back neck, k.20 sts. from holder, pick up and k.40 (41, 42) sts. up left back neck, 47 (48, 49) sts. down left front neck, k.20 sts. from holder, pick up and k.47 (48, 49) sts. up right front neck: 213 (217, 221) sts.

Starting rib row 2, work 3 rows rib as given for back.

Cast off in rib.

TO MAKE UP

Block and press pieces lightly under a damp cloth foll. ball band instructions. Join right shoulder and neckband seams. Join side seams. Join sleeve seams. Pin sleeves into armholes matching pattern. Sew in sleeves. Using lagon, work 'Half French knot' embroidery on lower fish as indicated on chart.

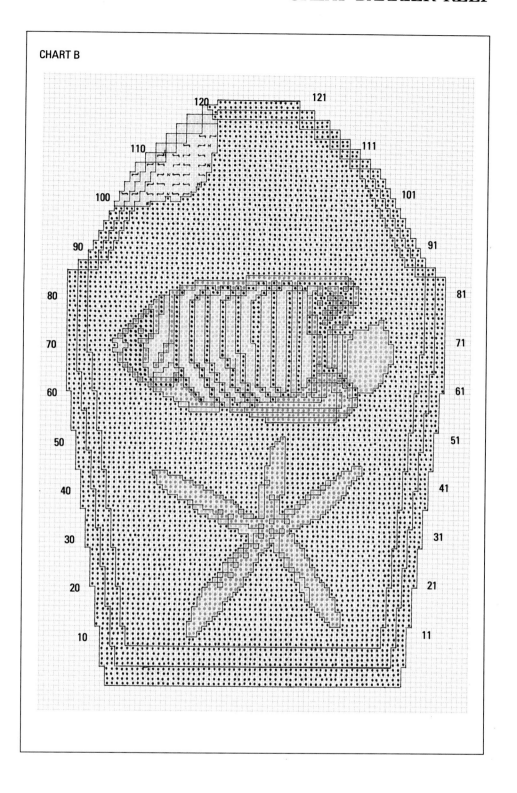

CHART B

Tallest of all land animals, Giraffes stalk the tropical savannahs and woodlands of Africa. Their great height not only allows them to browse in the tops of trees, but also helps them spot potential predators from a distance. Whilst this helps protect them from wild animals such as lions, it is less useful against man, and Giraffes have proved easy targets for hunters. They have been killed for food, for sport and for their skins and tails which are used to make fly-swatches. In western Africa, such killing and the loss of their habitat to agriculture and livestock raising has meant that Giraffes have become very rare. In East Africa, however, they are still common, particularly in national parks and game reserves such as the Serengeti National Park in Tanzania and the Amboseli Game Reserve in Kenya.

GIRAFFES
Browsing in the Savannah

▶ 'Tarzan meets Calamity Jane'. This safari suit has Western-style fringing and knitted patch pockets. The fringing represents the Giraffe's mane and the ribbed yoke gives the jacket a quilted look.

SIZES

Jacket

One size to fit 80–95cm – 32–38in bust.

Skirt

To fit 85 (90, 95)cm – 34 (36, 38)in hips, in two lengths

MATERIALS

Pingouin France + (used double)

Jacket

13 × 50g balls Ocre (shade 29)

4 × 50g balls Ecru (shade 17)

1 × 50g ball Noir (shade 29)

2.20m (2½yd) × 7.5cm (3in) fringing

5 × 2cm (¾in) and 2 × 1.5cm (⅝in) brass buttons.

Skirt

Mini version

4 (4, 5) × 50g balls Ocre (shade 29)

1 (1, 2) × 50g balls Ecru (shade 17)

Add one ball of each shade for longer length

80cm (⅞yd) or 95cm (1⅛yd) × 7.5cm (3in) fringing

15cm (6in) zip to match skirt

A pair each of 4mm (No. 8) and 4½mm (No. 7) knitting needles

Stitch holder

TENSION

16 sts. and 22 rows to 10cm over patt. worked on 4½mm needles

Check your tension

NOTES

Instructions for larger sizes are given in brackets ( ). When working pattern, use separate, small balls of yarn. When joining in a new colour, leave an end of about 5cm for darning in later. When changing colour, twist yarns together to avoid making a hole.

BACK

Using 4mm needles and ocre cast on 75 sts.

Rib row 1: K.1, * p.1, k.1; rep. from * to end.

Rib row 2: P.1, * k.1, p.1; rep. from * to end.

Rep. these 2 rows for 15 rows ending rib row 1.

Inc. row: Rib 8, m.1, * rib 6, m.1; rep. from * to last 7 sts., rib to end: 86 sts.

Change to 4½mm needles and work from row 17 of chart, setting patt. as folls:

Row 17: K.25 ocre, k.3 ecru, k.16 ocre, k.4 ecru, k.16 ocre, k.5 ecru, k.11 ocre, k.6 ecru.

'Giraffe' modelled by Mandy Smith. As a model Mandy graced the front covers of countless magazines. She now has a string of hit singles to her credit.

GIRAFFE

Cont. working from chart, shaping armholes by casting off 4 sts. at beg. of rows 77 and 78: 78 sts.

When row 86 of chart has been completed, using ocre work 2 rows dec. 1 st. at beg. of 2nd row: 77 sts.

Rib row 1: K.1 , * p.1, k.1; rep. from * to end.

Rib row 2: P.1, k.1, * yfwd, sl.1 purlwise, k.1; rep. from * to last st., p.1.

Rib row 3: K.1 , p.1, * k.1 tog. with sl.st., p.1; rep. from * to last st., k.1. Rep. rib rows 2 and 3 until 41 rows of rib have been worked, ending rib row 3.

Shape back neck

Working in rib as set, rib 29 sts., turn and leave rem. sts. on a stitch holder.

Next row: Cast off 5 sts., rib to end: 24 sts.

Rib 1 row. Cast off in rib.

Return to sts. on holder, with WS facing, slip first 19 sts. on a holder.

Rejoin yarn to rem. sts. and rib to end. Complete 2nd side of back neck to match first side, reversing all shaping.

LEFT FRONT

Using 4mm needles and ocre, cast on 43 sts.

Work 15 rows rib as given for back ending rib row 1.

Inc. row: Rib 13, m.1, * rib 4, m.1; rep from * to last 6 sts., rib 6: 50 sts.

Change to 4½mm needles and work from row 17 of chart placing patt. as folls:

Row 17: K.25 ocre, k.3 ecru, k.15 ocre, turn and leave rem. 7 sts. on a holder. Work on these 43 sts. only from row 18 to row 76 of chart.

Shape armhole

Cast off 4 sts. at beg. of row 77: 39 sts.

** When row 86 of chart has been completed, using ocre work 2 rows.

Now work 3 rib rows as given for jacket back yoke, then rep. rows 2 and 3 ** until 28 rib rows have been completed, ending rib row 2.

*** *Next row:* Rib in patt. to last 7 sts., turn and leave rem. sts. on a holder.

Work on these sts. only.

Dec. 1 st. at neck edge only on every row until 24 sts. rem. Work 7 rows straight.

Cast off in rib. ***

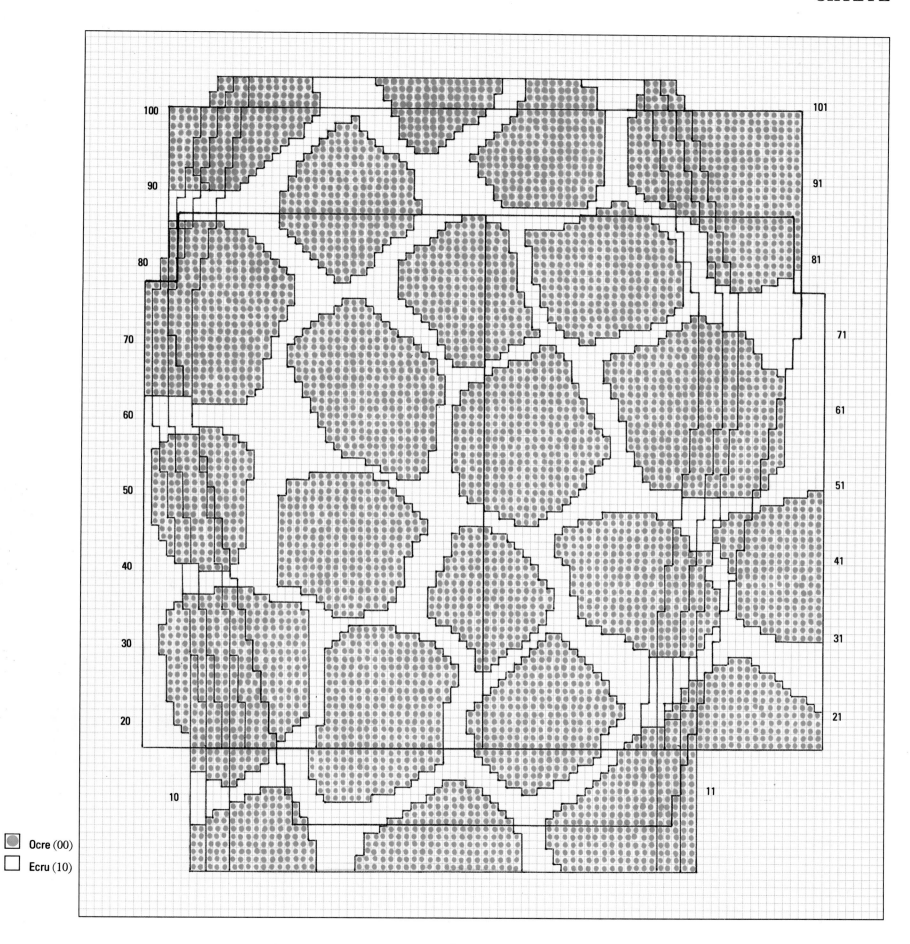

100

90

80

70

60

50

40

30

20

10

101

91

81

71

61

51

41

31

21

11

Ocre (00)

Ecru (10)

GIRAFFE

RIGHT FRONT

Using 4mm needles and ocre, cast on 43 sts.

Work 6 rows rib as given for back.

Next row: Rib 2, cast off 2 sts., rib to end.

Next row: Rib 39, turn, cast on 2 sts., turn, rib to end.

Work 7 more rows rib.

Inc. row: rib 6, m.1, * rib 4, m.1, rep. from * to last 13 sts., rib 6 sts., turn and leave rem. 7 sts. on a holder: 43 sts.

Change to 4½mm needles and work from centre point of row 17 of chart, setting patt. as folls.:

Row 17: K.1 ocre, k.4 ecru, k.16 ocre, k.5 ecru, k.11 ocre, k.6 ecru. Cont. working from chart shaping armhole by casting off 4 sts. at beg of row 78: 39 sts.

Now work as given for left front from ** to ** until 29 rib rows have been completed, ending rib row 3.

Complete by working from *** to *** as given for left front.

SLEEVES

Using 4mm needles and ocre, cast on 37 sts.

Work 6.5cm in k.1, p.1 rib as given for back, ending with rib row 1.

Inc. row: * Rib 3, m.1; rep. from * to last 4 sts., rib to end: 48 sts.

Change to 4½mm needles and work from row 7 of chart, placing patt. as folls.:

Row 7: K.16 ocre, k.4 ecru, k.16 ocre, k.10 ecru, k.2 ocre.

Cont. working from chart, at the same time, shape sides by inc. 1 st. each end of 5th and every foll. 4th row until there are 80 sts. Work 29 rows straight.

Cast off.

BUTTONBAND

Using 4mm needles and ocre with RS of left front facing, join yarn to first stitch on holder.

Work 100 rows in k.1, p.1 rib as given for back.

Leave sts. on a stitch holder.

Stitch buttonband to left front using invisible seam.

BUTTONHOLE BAND

Using 4mm needles and ocre, with WS of right front facing, join yarn to first stitch on holder.

Starting rib row 2, work in k.1, p.1 rib as given for back until 24 rows have been worked from last buttonhole.

Next row: Rib 2, cast off 2 sts., rib to end.

Next row: Rib 3, turn, cast on 2 sts., turn, rib to end.

* Rib 24 rows, then work 2 buttonhole rows, rep. from * until 5 buttonholes have been worked.

Rib 4 rows, leave sts. on holder.

Join buttonhole band to right front using invisible seam.

NECKBAND

Join shoulder seams.

Using 4mm needles and ocre, with RS facing, k. across 7 sts. of buttonhole band, 7 sts. of right front, pick up and k.15 sts. up right front neck, 7 sts. at right back neck, 19 sts. at back neck, 7 sts. at left back neck, 15 sts. at left front neck, k. across 7 sts. of left front and 7 sts. of buttonband: 91 sts.

Cast off all sts.

COLLAR

Using 4mm needles and ocre, cast on 83 sts. Work 20 rows in k.1, p.1 rib as given for back welt. Cast off in rib. Starting at 5th st. on left front, with WS tog., join collar to neck, matching cast off edges, stitch by stitch.

POCKETS (Knit 2)

Using 4½mm needles and noir, cast on 20 sts.

Beg. with a k. row, work 23 rows st.st.

Row 24: Knit.

Row 25: Purl.

Row 26: K.2, k.2 tbl, k. to last 4 sts., k.2 tog., k.2.

Row 27: P.2, p.2 tog., p. to last 4 sts., p.2 tog. tbl, p.2.

Rep. rows 26 and 27 until 4 sts. rem.

Next row: K.2 tog. tbl, k.2 tog.

Next row: P.2 tog., break yarn, pull through.

TO MAKE UP

Block and press pieces lightly under a damp cloth foll. ball band instructions. Fold and press pocket flap to right side. Stitch point in place and sew on a small button. Position pockets by placing top edge just below ribbed yoke. Slipstitch or machine stitch in place. Backstitch or machine length of fringing across back just below ribbed yoke and round each armhole where ribbing begins and ends. Join side seams. Sew sleeve seams and cover seams with fringing from top of cuff to armhole. Pin sleeves in place, matching fringed sleeve seam to back yoke fringing. Sew in place. Sew on buttons.

Skirt

BACK AND FRONT

Longer length

Using 4mm needles and ecru, cast on 63 (69, 73) sts.

Work 5 rows in k.1, p.1 rib as given for jacket back.

Change to 4½mm needles.

Dec. row: P.3 (1, 3), p.2 tog., * p.5 (6, 6), p.2 tog., rep. from * to last 2 (2, 4) sts., p. to end: 54 (60, 64) sts.

Now work from row 1 of chart, placing patt. as folls.:

Row 1: K.12 (15, 17) ocre, k.5 ecru, k.21 ocre, k.5 ecru, k.11 (14,16) ocre.

Cont. working from chart, at the same time inc. 1 st. each end of row 35 ** and every foll. 6th row until there are 64 (70, 74) sts.

Work 17 rows straight.

Now dec.1 st. each end of next and every foll. 4th row until 50 (56, 60) sts. rem.

2nd and 3rd sizes only

P.1 row, then dec. 1 st. at each end of last row. 50 (54, 58) sts.

All sizes

Work 3 (1, 1) rows in patt., dec 1 st. at end of last row: 49 (53, 57) sts.

Change to 4mm needles and using ocre, work 6.5cm in k.1, p.1 rib as given for jacket back welt. **

Mini length

Using 4mm needles and ecru, cast on 59 (65, 69) sts.

Work 5 rows in k.1, p.1 rib as given for jacket back.

Change to 4½mm needles.

Dec. row: P.5 (3, 1), p.2 tog., * p.4 (5, 6), p.2 tog.; rep. from * to last 4 (4, 2) sts., p. to end: 50 (56, 60) sts.

Now work from row 17 of chart, placing patt. as folls.:

Row 17: K.2 (5, 7) ocre, k.3 ecru, k.16 ocre, k.4 ecru, k.16 ocre, k.5 ecru, k.4 (7, 9) ocre.

Cont. working from chart, at the same time, inc. 1 st. each end of row 25.

Now work as given for longer length from ** to **.

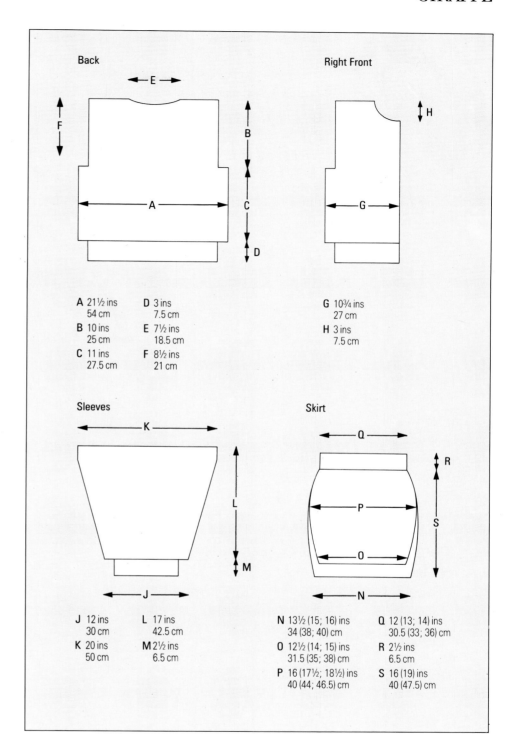

A	21½ ins 54 cm	D	3 ins 7.5 cm	
B	10 ins 25 cm	E	7½ ins 18.5 cm	
C	11 ins 27.5 cm	F	8½ ins 21 cm	

G	10¾ ins 27 cm
H	3 ins 7.5 cm

J	12 ins 30 cm	L	17 ins 42.5 cm
K	20 ins 50 cm	M	2½ ins 6.5 cm

N	13½ (15; 16) ins 34 (38; 40) cm	Q	12 (13; 14) ins 30.5 (33; 36) cm
O	12½ (14; 15) ins 31.5 (35; 38) cm	R	2½ ins 6.5 cm
P	16 (17½; 18½) ins 40 (44; 46.5) cm	S	16 (19) ins 40 (47.5) cm

TO MAKE UP

Block and press pieces lightly under a damp cloth foll. ball band instructions. Join side seams leaving 15cm on left side for zip. Insert zip. Sew fringing along side seams, from top of hem to base of waistband.

There are three species of Zebra, all of them found in Africa. The most familiar is the stocky Plains or Common Zebra which is still abundant on the grasslands and savannahs of East Africa. Less well known and rarer are the Mountain Zebra of south-west Africa and the elegant Grevy's Zebra of southern Somalia and Ethiopia and northern Kenya. Mountain Zebras have been intensively persecuted by farmers who thought that they competed with domestic livestock for grazing and water. Numbers were reduced from over 70,000 in the 1950s to around 7,000 by the end of the 1970s. Fortunately the remaining Mountain Zebras are relatively well protected in several different national parks and reserves. Much less secure is Grevy's Zebra, which has suffered badly from hunting and from prolonged droughts. Few Grevy's Zebras are protected in reserves and their numbers are still decreasing.

Burchells
ZEBRA

▶ The 'Modernist' arrangement of the Zebra stripes lends itself so readily to textile design. This easy-to-make outfit in cotton uses the stripes on the skirt and the yoke of the sweater. The fringing represents the Zebra's thick black mane.

SIZES
Sweater:
to fit 80 (85/90, 95)cm – 32 (34/36, 38)in bust
Skirt:
82.5 (87.5, 92.5)cm – 33 (35, 37)in hips.

MATERIALS
Pingouin Corrida 4 (DK cotton)
Sweater
11 × 50g balls Blanc (shade 501)
2 × 50g balls Noir (shade 528)
2.10m (2¼yd) of black fringing
4 × 1.5cm (⅝ in) white buttons
Skirt
5 × 50g balls Blanc (shade 501)
2 × 50g balls Noir (shade 528)
15cm (6 in) white zip
A pair each of 3¼mm (No. 10) and 4mm (No. 8) knitting needles
Stitch holder

TENSION
20 sts. and 26 rows to 10cm over patt. worked on 4mm needles
Check your tension

NOTES
Instructions for larger sizes are given in brackets ( ). When working pattern, use separate, small balls of yarn for each black and white area. This will avoid looping or weaving the yarn and will keep the tension more even. When joining in a new colour, leave an end of about 5cm for darning in later. When changing colour, twist yarns together at back of work to avoid making a hole.

Sweater

BACK
** Using 3¼mm needles and blanc, cast on 93 (97, 101) sts.
Rib row 1: K.1, * p.1, k.1; rep from * to end.
Rib row 2: P.1 , * k.1, p.1; rep. from * to end.
Rep. these 2 rows once, inc. 1 st. at end of last row: 94 (98, 102) sts.
Change to 4mm needles and work 34 (36, 38) rows st.st.

'Burchells Zebra' modelled by Caron Keating, co-presenter of Blue Peter, *the popular BBC children's programme. Swimming with sharks in the Pacific Ocean and with wild dolphins off the coast of Ireland have been two of Caron's amazing assignments for* Blue Peter.

ZEBRA

Shape armholes

Cast off 4 sts.at beg. of next 2 rows: 86 (90, 94) sts.

Work 4 (8, 8) rows straight, then 2 rows noir.

Now work from row 51 of chart **.

Joining in small balls of colour, set pattern as follows:

Row 51: K.6 (8, 10) blanc, k.4 noir, 3 blanc, 6 noir, 2 blanc, 4 noir, 5 blanc, 4 noir, 4 blanc, 5 noir, 7 blanc, 5 noir, 2 blanc, 1 noir, 7 blanc, 2 noir, 17 blanc, 1 noir, 1 (3, 5) blanc.

Continue until row 100 has been completed.

Shape back neck

Next row: Working in pattern, k.33 (35, 37) sts., turn and leave rem. sts. on a stitch holder.

Work on these sts. only.

Next row: Cast off 4 sts., p. to end.

K.1 row.

Cast off 3 (4, 4) sts., p. to end.

Cast off.

Return to rem. sts.

With RS facing, slip first 20 sts. onto a stitch holder.

Rejoin yarn and k. to end.

Now complete to match first side, reversing all shaping.

FRONT

Work as given for back from ** to **

Divide for front opening

Joining in small balls of colour, work left half of Chart from row 51, setting patt. as follows:

Row 51: K.6 (8, 10) blanc, 4 noir, 3 blanc, 6 noir, 2 blanc, 4 noir, 5 blanc, 4 noir, 4 blanc, 2 noir, turn and leave rem. sts. on a stitch holder: 40 (42, 44) sts.

Work in pattern on these sts. only for left front until row 92 has been completed.

Shape left front neck

Next row: K.33 (35, 37) sts., turn and leave rem. 7 sts. on a holder.

Dec. 1 st. at neck edge only until 26 (27, 29) sts. rem.

Work 4 (3, 3) rows straight.

Cast off.

Return to sts. for right front.

With RS facing and using blanc, rejoin yarn and cast off first 6 sts. Following right half of Chart from row 51, work

in patt. to end: 40 (42, 44) sts. Continue in pattern from chart until row 93 has been completed.

Shape right front neck

Next row: P.33 (35, 37) sts., turn and leave rem. 7 sts. on a stitch holder.

Now complete to match left front, reversing all shaping.

SLEEVES

Using 3¼mm needles and blanc, cast on 47 (51, 51) sts.

Work 17 rows in rib as given for back.

Inc. row: (WS) Rib 3 (5, 5), m.1, * rib 5, m.1; rep. from * to last 4 (6, 6) sts., rib to end: 56 (60, 60) sts.

Change to 4mm needles and work in st.st., inc. 1 st. at each end of 5th and every foll. 4th row until there are 96 (100, 100) sts.

Cont. straight until work measures 47.5 (50.5, 51) cm from beg. of sleeve.

Cast off.

BUTTONBAND

Using 3¼mm needles and blanc, with RS facing, pick up and k.29 sts.along left front. P.1 row.

Work 8 rows in rib as given for back.

Cast off in rib.

BUTTONHOLE BAND

Using 3¼mm needles and blanc, with RS facing, pick up and k.29 sts. along right front. P.1 row

Work 4 rows in rib as given for back.

Next row: Rib 7, yrn, k.2 tog, * rib 6, yrn, k.2 tog.; rep from * to last 4 sts.

Rib to end.

Work 3 more rows in rib.

Cast off in rib.

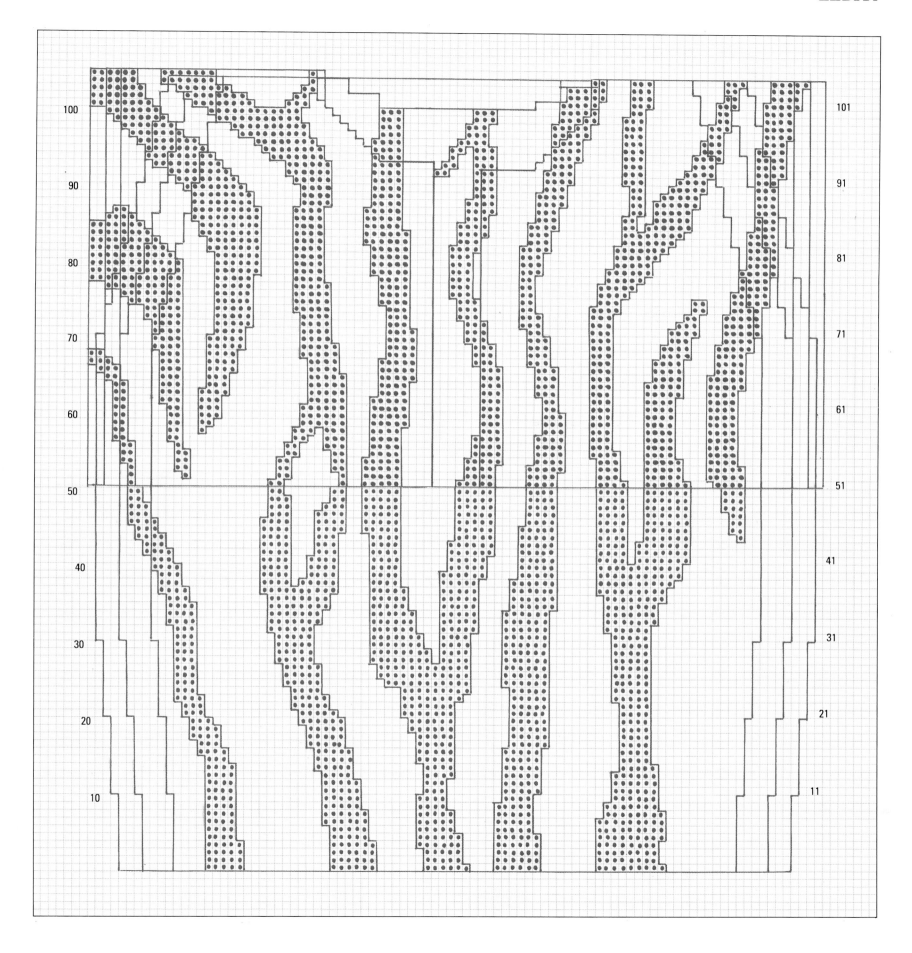

NECKBAND

Join both shoulder seams.

Using 3¼mm needles and blanc, with RS facing, pick up and k.8 sts. across buttonhole band, k.7 sts. from holder, pick up and k.12 (13, 13) sts. up right front neck, 10 (11, 11) sts. down right back neck, k.20 sts. from holder, pick up and k.10 (11, 11) sts. up left back neck, 13 (14, 14) sts. down left front neck, k. 7 sts. from holder, pick up and k.8 sts. across buttonband: 95 (99, 99) sts.

P.1 row.

Cast off.

COLLAR

Using 3¼mm needles and blanc, cast on 95 (99, 99) sts.

Work 22 rows in rib as given for back.

Next row: Rib 3, yrn, k.2 tog., rib to end.

Work 3 rows rib.

Cast off in rib.

TO MAKE UP

Block and press pieces lightly under a damp cloth following ball band instructions. Stitch buttonhole band and buttonband to cast off sts. at centre front. Machine or backstitch fringing across front and back yokes, stitching across 2 rows noir, and around armhole edge of yokes. Stitch cast off edge of collar to neckband. Joining cast off edge of armhole to underarms, sew in sleeves, then join side and sleeve seams, sew on buttons.

Skirt (Back and front alike)

Using 3¼mm needles and blanc, cast on 83 (91, 97) sts.

Work 6 rows rib as given for sweater back.

Change to 4mm needles.

Dec. row: P.5 (5, 7), p.2 tog., * p.5 (6, 6), p.2 tog.; rep. from * to last 6 (4, 8) sts., p. to end: 72 (80, 86) sts.

Work rows 1–104 from chart, shaping sides as shown: 60 (68, 74) sts.

Next row: Using blanc, k.2 tog., k. to end: 59 (67, 73) sts.

Change to 3¼mm needles and starting with rib row 2 as given for sweater back, work 5cm in k.1, p.1 rib.

Cast off in rib.

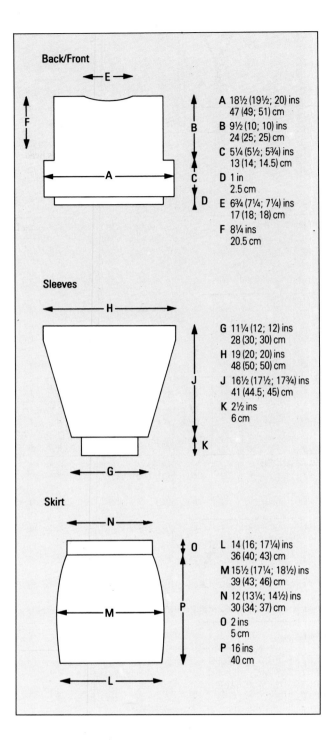

Back/Front

A 18½ (19½; 20) ins
47 (49; 51) cm

B 9½ (10; 10) ins
24 (25; 25) cm

C 5¼ (5½; 5¾) ins
13 (14; 14.5) cm

D 1 in
2.5 cm

E 6¾ (7¼; 7¼) ins
17 (18; 18) cm

F 8¼ ins
20.5 cm

Sleeves

G 11¼ (12; 12) ins
28 (30; 30) cm

H 19 (20; 20) ins
48 (50; 50) cm

J 16½ (17½; 17¾) ins
41 (44.5; 45) cm

K 2½ ins
6 cm

Skirt

L 14 (16; 17¼) ins
36 (40; 43) cm

M 15½ (17¼; 18½) ins
39 (43; 46) cm

N 12 (13¼; 14½) ins
30 (34; 37) cm

O 2 ins
5 cm

P 16 ins
40 cm

TO MAKE UP

Block and press pieces lightly under a damp cloth following ball band instructions. Join side seams leaving an opening of 15cm on left side seam. Sew in zip using machine or backstitch.

YARN SUPPLIERS

	PATONS	EMU	PINGOUIN	HAYFIELD
UK	Patons & Baldwins Ltd Alloa Clackmannanshire EK10 TEG Scotland Beehive softblend DK	Emu International Ltd Leeds Road Idle Bradford West Yorkshire BD10 9TE	Pingouin French Wools Ltd Station House 81–83 Fulham High St. London SW6 3JW	Hayfield Hayfield Textiles Ltd Glusburn Keighley West Yorkshire BD20 8QP
CANADA	Patons & Baldwins Ltd 1001 Rost Lawn Avenue Toronto Beehive DK	S. R. Kertzer Ltd 105A Winges Road Woodbridge, Ontario L4L 6C2, Canada	1500 Rue Jules Poitras Ville St. Laurent, Quebec, Canada	Mr K. Ehman Craftsmen Distributors Inc 4166 Halifax Street Burnaby British Columbia V5C 3XC
AUSTRALIA	Coats & Patons Pty Ltd 89–91 Peters Avenue Mulgrave Victoria 3170 Australia Beehive 8-ply	Karingal Vic/Tas Pty Ltd 6 Macro Court Rowville Victoria 3178 Australia	47–57 Collins St Alexandria New South Wales 2015 or PO Box 163 Beaconsfield New South Wales 2014	Karingal (Emu supplier) Vic Tas Pty Ltd 359 Dorset Road Bayswater, Victoria 3153
NEW ZEALAND	Coats & Patons (NZ) Ltd 263 Ti Rakau Drive Pakuranga Auckland N2 Beehive 8-ply	Enzed Sewing Ltd 40 Sir William Avenue East Tamaki Auckland, PO Box 61–087 New Zealand	Not available see substitution chart or contact Australian supplier.	Not available. For details see Australia
SOUTH AFRICA	Not available: See substitution chart	Brasen Hobby PO Box 6405 Johannesburg 2000 South Africa	Pingouin Yarns Saprotex (Pty) Ltd PO Box 306, New Germany 3620 South Africa	Brasch Hobby (Emu supplied) 57 La Rochelle Road Trojan Johannesburg 2197

YARN SUBSTITUTION

If you have any difficulty in obtaining all the shades recommended in the patterns, please use this simple guide to substitute yarns:

GARMENTS	YARN SUBSTITUTES	GARMENTS	YARN SUBSTITUTES
BADGER/WILD FLOWERS GIANT PANDAS ORCAS–KILLER WHALES BLACK RHINO	Any thick, chunky yarns e.g. *Emu* Snowball, *Patons* Parade, *Hayfield* Grampian Chunky, and *Emu* Supermatch Chunky with *Emu* Supermatch DK.	GT. BARRIER REEF ZEBRA SWANS/DAFFODILS	Any DK Cotton or Cotton-mix eg. *Pingouin* Cotonade, Coton Mercerise no. 4; *Patons* Cotton Perle, Cotton Soft or Baby Cotton; *Schachenmayr* Alpha; *ScheepJeswol* Mayflower DK.
POLAR BEARS GIRAFFE	Any Aran, or softer chunky yarns eg. *Hayfield* Grampian Aran, *Hayfield* Brig Aran, *Patons* Diploma Aran, *Emu* Supermatch Chunky.	MOUNTAIN GORILLA	Any Mohair yarns eg. *Emu* Filigree; *Patons* Mohair Visions; *Pingouin* Mohair or Pidou. Any Chunky yarns eg. *Emu* Supermatch Chunky; *Patons* Parade.
INDIAN/WHITE TIGERS LIONESSES GOLDEN EAGLE BABY SEAL AFRICAN ELEPHANT	Any DK 100% wool or wool-mix yarns eg. *Pingouin* '4 Pingouins', Confort, France +, Challenge 4, Pure Laine no. 4; *Patons* Beehive or Diploma; *Hayfield* Grampian DK; *Emu* Supermatch DK; *Schachenmayr* Extra		Please remember to *check your tensions*, when substituting yarns, and adjust needle size accordingly.

KNITTING KNOW-HOW

ABBREVIATIONS

k.	knit
p.	purl
st(s).	stitch(es)
st.st.	stocking stitch
rev.st.st.	reversed stocking stitch
patt.	pattern
rep.	repeat
beg.	beginning
inc.	increase(ing)
dec.	decrease(ing)
tog.	together
sl.	slip
in	inch(es)
mm	millimetres
cm	centimetres
psso	pass slip stitch over
m.1	make one
RS	right side
WS	wrong side
tbl	through back of loop
dc.	double crochet

READING CHARTS

The patterns in this book all use charts. Each chart consists of a grid, sometimes the piece being knitted into the actual shape marked up in the squares. Each square represents one stitch and each horizontal line of squares represents one row.

Unless otherwise given out in the instructions the design as shown on the chart is worked in stocking stitch, all odd numbered rows being read from right to left and worked as knit stitches (right-side rows) and all even numbered rows being read from left to right and worked as purl stitches (wrong-side rows).

Each square shows which colour yarn is to be used for that stitch.

If on the design you are working there is only a small motif to be worked, then the chart is only given for that area of the sweater and the instructions will tell you where to place the motif within the row. All stitches either side of the chart are then worked in the main colour.

If the chart is for the full section of the piece you are knitting, then it will usually indicate any shaping that needs to be done. If the number of squares varies at the side, armhole and neck edges, then increase or decrease that number of stitches at that point on the row you are working.

At the centre front neck, where there are usually quite a few to be shaped, either leave the centre stitches on a holder or refer to the pattern instructions to see if it tells you to cast them off.

CHANGING COLOURS

When working from the charts it is necessary to use several different colours, very often within the same row.

If there are very small areas to be worked in any of the colours, then wind off a small amount of yarn either into a small ball or onto a bobbin. This will make working with a lot of colours easier and help to stop them getting muddled. When joining in a new colour at the beginning of a row, insert the needle into the first stitch, make a loop in the new yarn, leaving an end to be later darned in, then place this loop over the needle and complete the stitch.

When joining in a new colour in the middle of a row, work in the first colour to the point where the new colour is needed, then insert the needle into the next stitch and complete with the new colour in the same way as for joining in at the beginning of a row.

When changing colour along a row always make sure that the colour that is being used is twisted around the next colour to be used, otherwise the two stitches willl not be linked together and a hole will form between them.

FINISHING

After knitting all the pieces for the garment, first darn in all the ends securely, then for a better finished look block out all the pieces.

Firstly cover a large area with a thick blanket and a piece of clean fabric such as sheeting. Lay out each piece of the garment and pin out to shape.

If the yarn can be pressed then cover with a damp cloth and press each piece lightly avoiding all ribbing. Do not move the iron over the fabric, but keep picking up and placing it lightly down again.

If the yarn cannot be pressed then cover with a damp cloth and leave until completely dry.

EMBROIDERY

Some of the designs have added embroidery to give extra detail. The first of these is called Backstitch and this is used whenever a line is needed. The second stitch used is a French Knot and this is used whenever spots or dots are needed.

Backstitch

Thread the needle with the required coloured yarn and fasten at the back of the work.

Bring the needle through to the right side of the fabric.

Changing Colour

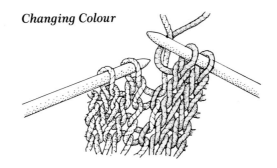

Backstitch

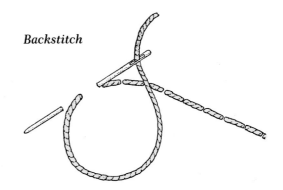

Insert the needle back through the fabric about 5mm to the right of where the yarn was brought through and then bring it back out again about 5mm to the left of the first stitch. Draw the needle through, pulling the yarn gently. Now insert the needle back into the fabric at the end of the first stitch and bring it out again 5mm further along. Continue in this way until the line has been completed, then fasten off securely.

French Knot and Half French Knot

Thread the needle with the required coloured yarn and fasten at the back of the work.

Bring the needle through to the right side of the fabric at the position for the knot. Take a small stitch of the fabric and wind the yarn twice round the point of the needle for a french knot and once for a half french knot. Pull the needle carefully through the fabric at the base of the knot and fasten off on the wrong side.

French Knot

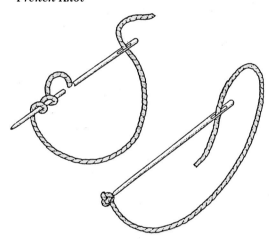

MAKING UP

Once the pieces have been finished refer to the making up instructions for the order in which to assemble them. When joining seams where the pattern needs to match at any point then the invisible seam method gives a more professional finish, but a backstitched seam is slightly easier and with care can give just as neat a finish.

Invisible seam

Lay both pieces of fabric to be joined on a flat surface with the right side facing. Thread the needle with matching yarn and join it to the lower edge of one of the pieces.

Take the needle and insert it into the centre of the first stitch at the lower edge of the second piece of knitting.

Invisible Seam

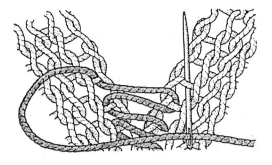

Bring the needle back up through the stitch above, so picking up the bar between the rows of stitches. Pull the yarn through, then take the needle back across to the first piece of knitting and repeat. Pull the yarn gently so that the two pieces of knitting are drawn together. Insert the needle back into the second piece of knitting, in the same place as the needle came out, and pick up the next bar above, then repeat again on the first piece of knitting. Continue in this way to the top of the seam, gently pulling the yarn every few stitches to close the seam.

After the last stitch fasten off securely.

Backstitch seam

Place the two pieces to be joined right sides together.

Thread the needle with matching yarn.

Bring the needle through to the right side of the fabric

Backstitch Seam

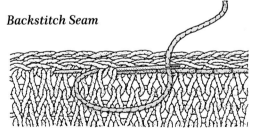

and fasten to the beginning of the seam with a couple of stitches.

Insert the needle through both thicknesses and bring it back out again about 5mm along the seam. Draw the needle through, pulling the yarn gently. Insert the needle back into

the same place as it was inserted the first time but this time bring it out about 5mm further along from the last stitch. Pull the yarn through.

Now insert the needle back into the fabric at the end of the first stitch and bring it out again 5mm further along. Continue in this way to the end of the seam, then fasten off securely.

Swiss Darning

Thread the needle with the required coloured yarn and fasten at the back of the work.

Bring the needle through to the right side of the fabric through the centre of the lower point of the stitch. Insert the needle at the top right hand side of the same stitch. Hold the needle in a horizontal position and draw it through the top left hand side of the stitch. Now insert again into the base of the stitch to the left of where the needle came out at the start of the stitch. Keep the yarn loose enough to lie on top of the work and cover the knitted stitch.

Swiss Darning

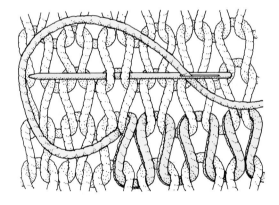

AFTERCARE

After all the hard work of knitting and making up your garment it is important to wash it correctly in order to keep it looking as new.

Always keep a ball band from one of the balls of yarn that the garment was knitted with, so that you can always refer to the washing instructions for that yarn. If there are no washing instructions on the ball band, or if you have not kept one, then hand wash only in cool water. Either squeeze gently or give a short spin, then lay the garment flat and ease into shape. Dry flat away from heat or direct sunlight.

ACKNOWLEDGEMENTS

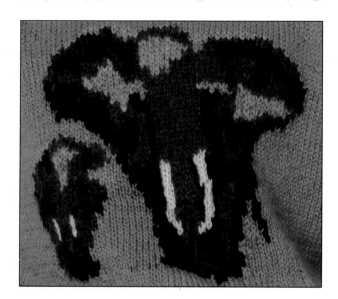

Ruth and Karen would like to thank everyone involved in the book, especially our wonderful models.

Kim Knott and his studio assistant, Nick Pearson.

Jane Cohen, Celia Hunter, Mary Vango, Lino of Gelrard and Lino, Charlie Green and special thanks to Keith at Smile for Marie Helvin's hair.

Winifred Muir, Christine Kingdom, Margaret Slater, Debbie Hudson, Sandra Cook and Rose for their enthusiasm and efficiency in supplying yarn.

Our knitters: Dorothy Herring, Sue Williams, Olwyn Webb, Auntie Dorothy, June and Margaret.